'This book succinctly and concisely outlines the Mental Capacity Act for professionals who work in education. Practical suggestions, further reading and how the Mental Capacity Act fits into wider Special Educational Needs and Disability reforms are offered, discussed and illustrated through authentic scenarios.'

– *Dr Nazam Hussain, Educational Psychologist*

'This book is clear and informative. It offers practical examples to develop the reader's understanding of the importance of the Mental Capacity Act and its interplay with the SEND Code of Practice. It should be essential reading for education staff and Local Authority staff, including SEN officers, as well as social service staff and health professionals who work with children and young people in educational contexts from Key Stage 4 onwards.'

– *Karen Flanagan, County SEN Manager (Assessment and Placement), Kent County Council of related interest*

**Restorative Practice and Special Needs**
**A Practical Guide to Working Restoratively with Young People**
*Nick Burnett and Margaret Thorsborne*
*Foreword by Nancy Riestenberg*
ISBN 978 1 84905 543 7
eISBN 978 0 85700 968 5

**Personalisation in Practice**
**Supporting Young People with Disabilities through the Transition to Adulthood**
*Suzie Franklin and Helen Sanderson*
*Foreword by Nicola Gitsham*
ISBN 978 1 84905 443 0
eISBN 978 0 85700 816 9

# Applying the Mental Capacity Act 2005 in Education

A Practical Guide for
EDUCATION PROFESSIONALS

**JANE L. SINSON**

Jessica Kingsley *Publishers*
London and Philadelphia

First published in 2016
by Jessica Kingsley Publishers
73 Collier Street
London N1 9BE, UK
and
400 Market Street, Suite 400
Philadelphia, PA 19106, USA

www.jkp.com

Copyright © Jane L. Sinson 2016

All rights reserved. No part of this publication may be reproduced in any material form (including photocopying or storing it in any medium by electronic means and whether or not transiently or incidentally to some other use of this publication) without the written permission of the copyright owner except in accordance with the provisions of the Copyright, Designs and Patents Act 1988 or under the terms of a licence issued by the Copyright Licensing Agency Ltd, Saffron House, 6–10 Kirby Street, London EC1N 8TS. Applications for the copyright owner's written permission to reproduce any part of this publication should be addressed to the publisher.

Warning: The doing of an unauthorised act in relation to a copyright work may result in both a civil claim for damages and criminal prosecution.

**Library of Congress Cataloging in Publication Data**
Names: Sinson, Jane L., author.
Title: Applying the Mental Capacity Act 2005 in Education : a practical guide for education professionals / Jane L. Sinson.
Description: London ; Philadelphia : Jessica Kingsley Publishers, [2016] | Includes bibliographical references and index.
Identifiers: LCCN 2015035415 | ISBN 9781785920028 (alk. paper)
Subjects: LCSH: People with mental disabilities--Education--Great Britain. | Students with disabilities--Education--Great Britain. | Great Britain. Mental Capacity Act 2005. | Great Britain. Children and Families Act 2014. | Capacity and disability--Great Britain. | Youth--Legal status, laws, etc.--Great Britain.
Classification: LCC KD737 .S56 2016 | DDC 344.41/0791--dc23 LC record available at http://lccn.loc.gov/2015035415

**British Library Cataloguing in Publication Data**
A CIP catalogue record for this book is available from the British Library

ISBN 978 1 78592 002 8
eISBN 978 1 78450 240 9

Printed and bound in the United States

*In memory of my sister, who sometimes presented me with the real-life challenge of applying the Mental Capacity Act 2005.*

# Contents

ACKNOWLEDGEMENTS . . . . . . . . . . . . . . . . . . . . . . . . . . . 9

Prolegomenon  The Importance of the SEND COP
Annex 1 . . . . . . . . . . . . . . . . . . . . . . . . . . . . . . . 11

**PART 1**     **THE MENTAL CAPACITY ACT (MCA) 2005**

Chapter 1     Introduction . . . . . . . . . . . . . . . . . . . . . . . . . 19

Chapter 2     The MCA Five Principles . . . . . . . . . . . . . . . . . 29

Chapter 3     Mental Capacity and to Lack Capacity . . . . . . 51

**PART 2**     **ASSESSING A YOUNG PERSON'S MENTAL CAPACITY**

Chapter 4     'More Serious or Significant Decisions' . . . . . 61

Chapter 5     'Legal Consequences' Decisions:
Appealing to the SEND Tribunal . . . . . . . . . . 115

Chapter 6     Additional Considerations for Educational
Psychologists . . . . . . . . . . . . . . . . . . . . . . . . 129

**PART 3**     **EDUCATION PROFESSIONALS, THE YOUNG PERSON AND THEIR FAMILY**

Chapter 7     Resolving Disagreements about
the Outcome of a Mental
Capacity Assessment . . . . . . . . . . . . . . . . . . 145

Chapter 8     'Best Interests' and 'Best Interests'
Checklist . . . . . . . . . . . . . . . . . . . . . . . . . . . 151

Chapter 9     Supporting and Working with Parents . . . . . . 169

| Epilogue | Putting the MCA Principles and Processes into Practice. | 187 |
|---|---|---|
| | GLOSSARY | 193 |
| APPENDIX 1 | CAPACITY ASSESSMENT RECORD FORM | 197 |
| | Mental Capacity Act 2005 Capacity Assessment Record (MCAcar) | 204 |
| | Capacity assessment | 207 |
| | 'Four key questions' | 209 |
| | Capacity assessment ground rules | 218 |
| APPENDIX 2 | IDENTIFYING WHICH YOUNG PEOPLE MAY BE CONSIDERED TO LACK CAPACITY | 219 |
| APPENDIX 3 | 'BEST INTERESTS' | 221 |
| APPENDIX 4 | WHAT YOUNG PEOPLE CAN LEGALLY DO FROM THE AGE OF 16 | 229 |
| | REFERENCES | 231 |
| | RESOURCES | 235 |
| | INDEX | 243 |

# Acknowledgements

Grateful thanks are due to:

- The participants at the National Sensory Impairment Partnership (NatSIP) Mental Capacity Act (MCA) 2005 training days (October and November 2014) and working day (February 2015), whose thoughts and questions inspired the book, and for their help to develop an MCA capacity assessment record.

- Maureen Roberts, First-tier Special Educational Needs and Disability (SEND) Tribunal and Mental Health Review Tribunal Judge, for painstakingly proofreading the book, to ensure I had not erred in my interpretation of the relevant legislation.

- Liz Goldthorpe, retired First-tier SEND Tribunal Judge, for all her support and encouragement to write the book.

- Lindsey Rousseau MBE, NatSIP facilitator, for her never-ending support, advice and encouragement.

- Patricia Gore, Andrew Lockley and all the other First-tier SEND Tribunal Judges, who so patiently gave me the benefit of their legal knowledge.

- Margery Page, retired senior educational psychologist, for proofreading the chapter for educational psychologists, and her ever-wise advice.

- Members of the NatSIP Reference Group for their advice, proofreading and support.

- Ed Yeates, for reading selected chapters and advice.

- Gillian Lawrence of the Seashell Trust, for turning my scribbles into a flowchart.

- My family, friends and colleagues, for their support and understanding.

*Prolegomenon*

# The Importance of the SEND COP Annex 1

> *Ignorance of the law excuses no man; not that all men know the law, but because 'tis an excuse every man will plead, and no man can tell how to confute him.*
>
> (John Seldon, 'Table Talk' (1689), 1892 edn, p.99, Oxford Reference (1981))

- Are you an education professional, that is, a secondary school/post-16 teacher, tutor, special educational needs coordinator (SENCo), specialist teacher, local authority SEN officer, local authority officer managing personal budgets, educational psychologist (EP), or do you support the learning of students aged 16–25?

- Do you work with or support young people with SEN aged 16–25 (SEND COP, January 2015) in an educational setting?

If you answered 'Yes' to either of these questions, this book is essential reading for you. (If you are an education professional working in Wales, however, see the section 'Education professionals in Wales' later in this chapter for a discussion of the relevance of this book to you.)

Like most education professionals, you will have read the *Special Educational Needs and Disability Code of Practice: 0–25 years* (SEND COP) sections applying to your role, but probably overlooked Annex 1 at the back. Alternatively, if you have read Annex 1, you are doubtless none the wiser about the concepts, implications and your responsibilities. Thus, you may have missed that the SEND COP incorporates the Mental Capacity Act 2005 Code of Practice (MCA COP) for education professionals working with young people aged

16–25. This means that you *must* (statutory requirement) have regard to *both* the SEND COP *and* the MCA COP.

## The SEND COP is inadequate guidance on the legal requirements

Annex 1 is the only guidance given by the Department for Education (DfE) regarding education professionals' responsibilities in relation to the MCA. It is brief, incomplete and lacking any definitions or clear advice. The first paragraph wording implies, rather than explicitly states, that there is a *legal* requirement for education professionals working with young people aged 16 and over, to have regard to *both* the SEND COP *and* the MCA COP. It does indicate that the MCA COP 'provides guidance on how the MCA works on a day-to-day basis' (p.273), but advises incorrectly that the MCA COP is available from the Ministry of Justice website.[1]

Overall, the SEND COP is ambiguous about the requirement to follow the MCA COP when supporting young people making their own decisions. Therefore, it is unsurprising that many education professionals are unaware of the full implications of the MCA COP in relation to their duties under the SEND COP.

## Mental capacity

The MCA is the legislation, in England and Wales, giving *everyone* the right, once they are 16 years old, to make their own decisions. 'Mental capacity' is defined as the ability to make a decision – any decision – big or small. For example, this could be a decision about what to wear, what to eat, which college to attend, what course to study, or whether to request a personal budget.

There are various references in the SEND COP to 'mental capacity' (e.g. 1.8, 8.21, Annex 1) or to 'capacity' (e.g. 2.12, 8.21);

---

1 The MCA COP can be downloaded from www.gov.uk/government/publications/mental-capacity-act-code-of-practice, or purchased from some high street or online booksellers or from The Stationery Office at www.tsoshop.co.uk.

both terms relate to the MCA legal definition of 'mental capacity'. It is common practice to use the terms interchangeably, and so this approach is adopted in this book. The SEND COP does not provide the definition, but Annex 1 states that 'mental capacity has the same meaning as in the Mental Capacity Act (MCA) 2005' (SEND COP, p.273), thereby indicating that the education professional should follow the MCA COP to determine whether the young person has the 'mental capacity' to make a particular decision.

As well as defining 'mental capacity', the MCA COP sets out the four components of decision-making that have to be achieved for a young person to be considered to have the 'capacity' to make the particular decision. These relate to the young person's ability to understand and retain the relevant information, to weigh it to decide, and to communicate their choice. These four elements become the questions that form the basis of a capacity assessment. In the SEND COP Annex 1, these are referred to as the 'four key questions' (p.274).

## Capacity assessment

The SEND COP Annex 1 is extremely sketchy about a capacity assessment, and the information it provides is not wholly correct. Most importantly, it omits the criteria that *have to be met* before a young person *may be* considered to possibly lack capacity to make a particular decision. This omission has led to education professionals erroneously believing that all young people receiving support under the SEND COP may lack capacity. However, when the missing criteria are applied, it is evident that this is not the case and that it is only a small subset of young people supported through the SEND COP who may be considered to lack capacity to make a particular decision. This is discussed in detail in Chapter 4, including which young people are likely to meet the omitted criteria.

Overall, a capacity assessment must be rigorous and carefully follow the procedure set out in the MCA COP Chapter 4. This is because the outcome of a capacity assessment may deem the young person as being unable to make their own choice, thereby removing their human right to self-determination for this decision. This may sound a little dramatic, but the MCA is actually part of UK human rights legislation, and a capacity assessment is the formal process that is set out in the MCA and MCA COP to determine whether a young person is able to make their own decision. The young person, their family or another professional, can challenge the outcome of a capacity assessment. The person undertaking the assessment must be able to show they have followed the correct procedure. If a dispute cannot be resolved through the local dispute resolution process, the matter could be referred to the Court of Protection. Putting a capacity assessment into its legislative context emphasises the importance of undertaking this meticulously. Thus, it is essential that education professionals know when and how to undertake a capacity assessment, including keeping an accurate record of the process.

## Is this book essential reading?

This practical book aims to rectify the inadequacies of the SEND COP Annex 1, in straightforward language, supported by case studies, thereby facilitating education professionals' understanding of how the MCA, via the MCA COP, links to the SEND COP, the implications and ensuing responsibilities. It:

- explains the five principles of the MCA (see Chapter 2)
- defines what is meant by 'mental capacity' and 'to lack capacity' (see Chapter 3)
- presents a step-by-step guide to knowing when and how to undertake a capacity assessment (see Chapter 4)
- provides a sample of a completed capacity assessment record form (see Appendix 1)
- gives suggestions for ways in which education professionals can support parents with the transition of decision-making from them to their young person (see Chapter 9).

To get the best from this book, downloading or purchasing a copy of the *Mental Capacity Act 2005 Code of Practice* is strongly recommended. This is written in a simpler, more accessible style than the SEND COP.

## SEND COP

Since the SEND COP was initially published in June 2014, it has been republished twice following amendments, July 2014 and January 2015. All references in this book relate to the SEND COP published in January 2015, which came into force in April 2015.

## Case studies

The case studies used throughout the book have all been made up to illustrate points. Jill, Sam, the education professionals, parents and educational establishments are all fictitious.

## Education professionals in Wales

If you answered 'Yes' to either of the questions at the start of the chapter, this book may be useful as the SEN legislation is changing. Although this book is written to explain the responsibilities in relation to the English Children and Families Act 2014, and the accompanying *Special Educational Needs and Disability Code of Practice: 0–25 Years*, the *Draft Additional Learning Needs and Education Tribunal (Wales) Bill* (the Bill) (Welsh Government 2015) suggests it will be similar to the English legislation, including a new code of practice. Like the English law, the Bill extends the age range for young people with additional learning needs to receive support in an educational setting until the age of 25. It emphasises the participation of children and young people, and consideration of their views, as part of the planning process (Draft Explanatory Memorandum, July 2015, Welsh Government 2015).

In relation to the Tribunal Wales (Education), there are significant differences between Wales and England, most notably in the Welsh concept of a 'case friend'. The Bill sets out an intention to specify when a child or young person has to have a case friend. It would be reasonable to speculate that this will make some reference to a young person's (16–25 years) right to make their own decision being subject to their capacity to do so, as set out in the MCA, which applies in England and Wales. Like the Children and Families Act 2014, the Bill makes provision for parents who may lack capacity to make decisions, although, like the English law, it does not indicate who will make the judgement about a parent's capacity. Therefore, education professionals in Wales are likely to need to be familiar with the MCA in educational contexts, and this book will facilitate this. In Wales, Chapters 1–4, 6, 8, 9 and the Epilogue are relevant, Chapter 7 possibly, but this will depend on the details relating to situations when the young person should have a case friend.

# Part 1

# The Mental Capacity Act (MCA) 2005

*Chapter 1*

# Introduction

*No decision about my education, without me.*

(Adapted from a slogan from Department of Health 2012)

> 'I know this booklet is about capacity, but I think, as a parent, I would be a bit unclear about who would be gathering my child's views about what, when and how this fits in with me as the parent knowing my young person and feeling I know what they want.' (Parent)
>
> 'I don't think it hit me until page 5 that my 16-year-old child has a right to decide on their education and their views would have priority over my own.' (Parent)

These comments from parents, reading a draft of a parent guide to the Mental Capacity Act (MCA) 2005 in education, probably sum up the challenge of the MCA and its relationship with the Children and Families Act 2014. Sometimes there may be some awkwardness, but at their heart, both laws have the same values relating to enabling young people to become autonomous. For the young person, this interrelationship begins on their 16th birthday. From then, education professionals and the young person's parents must give the young person every support and opportunity to make their own decisions. This emphasis on independence may test both education professionals and parents. The MCA is uncompromising in engendering the belief in those working with young people with special educational needs (SEN), and their parents, that young people can make their own decisions. The Children and Families Act

2014 fully supports this and, from the end of Year 11 (Y11),[1] gives young people the right to make decisions about their Education, Health and Care Plan (EHC Plan).

Throughout this book, the term 'parent' has the same meaning as in the *Special Educational Needs and Disability Code of Practice: 0–25 Years* (SEND COP) (see the Glossary) – that is, any person who is a parent or who has parental responsibility for the young person.

Although the two laws share core principles, some of their terminology is not aligned. The first area to be resolved relates to whom the term 'young person' refers.

## The young person: a conundrum of age and the law

The term 'young person' requires clarification as its meaning differs between the MCA and the Children and Families Act 2014. The MCA applies from the age of 16, and refers to those aged 16–17 as 'young people'; from a person's 18th birthday, they are considered 'adults'.

The Children and Families Act 2014 spans the age range 0–25, and defines 'young person' as 'a person over compulsory school age (the end of the academic year in which they turn 16)' (SEND COP Glossary) and under 25. Whilst it may seem odd to refer to those who are legally adults as 'young people', it is aligned with the United Nations (UN) definition of a young person as being aged between 15 and 24, although the UN acknowledges that member states may vary in this.

The SEND COP explains that compulsory school age ends on the last Friday in June in the academic year (Y11) in which the young person becomes 16 (SEND COP Introduction i). From this date, the Children and Families Act 2014 gives young people the right to make their own decisions, rather than their parents, about educational matters covered by the Children and Families Act 2014; these are set out in the SEND COP (8.16) and relate to EHC Plans.

---

1 The last Friday in June, provided the young person has reached their 16th birthday.

Also from this time, the local authority and other agencies should usually communicate directly with the young person rather than their parents (SEND COP 1.8).

However, the MCA applies from the 16th birthday, which, for the majority of young people, will occur during Y11 and before the last Friday in June of that academic year. Young people in Y11 are part of a school community that is likely to offer pupils more than the academic curriculum. Most secondary schools have a range of clubs, sports activities, organised trips, concerts, charity fundraisers and special events, etc. The young person's participation in these is probably unrelated to provision for their SEN, and therefore falls outside the varied age of decision-making set by the Children and Families Act 2014. That is, if taking part in the activity is not part of an outcome or provision documented in the EHC Plan, it is probably not part of the young person's special educational provision. So for these activities it can be assumed that, when the young person has had their 16th birthday, they should be encouraged to make their own decisions about taking part. This accords with a core principle of the Children and Families Act 2014 about young people participating as fully as possible in decisions.

What constitutes special educational provision may occasionally be unclear. For example, if a 16-year-old Y11 pupil requires assistance to take part in a school event, such as a charity fundraiser, is this special educational provision or is it related to the Equality Act 2010? The conclusion reached may affect whether the young person can make their own decision about participation.

Consider this scenario:

> Sam is in Y11, and has just had his 16th birthday. He is the subject of an EHC Plan due to learning difficulties, and attends his local mainstream high school. Mr Khan, Sam's head of year, talks to Sam about taking part in the voluntary Y11 sponsored walk for Children in Need during the school day. Mr Khan explains the arrangements for the walk, including enlisting sponsors and collecting the money afterwards. Sam decides he would like to take part.

> Mr Khan suggests that Sam has a sixth form buddy to help him; Sam thinks this is a good idea and agrees. Mr Khan reminds Sam to let his parents know he is taking part.

In this scenario, Mr Khan has assumed that as Sam is 16 years old he can make his own decisions. This is appropriate as it upholds the first principle of the MCA – the presumption of capacity. Mr Khan has offered a 'buddy', but this could be regarded as Mr Khan fulfilling his obligations under the Equality Act 2010 rather than SEN provision. Similarly, if Mr Khan had arranged teaching assistant (TA) support, this also probably related to responsibilities under the Equality Act 2010. Are there circumstances when Sam's need for support to participate in the walk could be deemed as special educational provision? This would depend on whether taking part in the walk has been written into his EHC Plan.

Then consider this scenario:

> At Sam's Y10 annual review, in June, his parents have agreed a new outcome: 'Sam will be able to communicate with peers and adults in real-life situations.' Mrs Robinson (special educational needs coordinator, SENCo) talked about the Y11 Children in Need sponsored walk, taking place in October, as a possible activity to develop Sam's communication skills in a real-life situation. Sam's parents agreed to him participating, as they felt it would give him an opportunity to talk with adults and peers to enlist sponsors and then collecting the money, as well as interacting with people during the walk. When asked his views, Sam was uncertain about being able to ask people to sponsor him, or to collect the money afterwards. He knew he could do the walk, but was worried about following the route by himself. Mrs Robinson suggested that Mr Smith (TA) could assist him; Sam accepted this would help him. The new outcome and participation in the sponsored walk with TA support were submitted as amendments to Sections E (outcomes) and F (provision)

> of the EHC Plan. Mrs Robinson suggested holding Sam's Y11 annual review during the first week of July, as Sam would then be able to make his own decisions about outcomes, provision and educational placement.
> 
> The local authority issued an amended EHC Plan in August ready for Y11. Sam's 16th birthday is 28 September; the walk is scheduled for 18 October.

Here Sam's participation in the sponsored walk forms part of his special educational provision as set out in Section F (special educational provision) of his EHC Plan. It was a decision made by his parents, when Sam was too young to be formally allowed to make his own choices, although his views were sought. Even though his 16th birthday precedes the walk, the Children and Families Act 2014 does not allow him to make his own decisions about his special educational provision until the end of Y11. Therefore, in this case, Sam's parents' decision stands, and he is not able to decide about his participation in the walk.

The Children and Families Act 2014 ensures close cooperation between education, health and social care. Between the ages of 16 and 17, a young person will have differing experiences of being able to make their own decisions. The Children Act 1989, which relates to social care (social workers), states that young people are able to make their own decisions from age 17. Healthcare professionals involve young people in making decisions about care and treatment from their 16th birthday. A young person, who is the subject of an EHC Plan, with provision in all sections, is likely to find different expectations of their involvement in decision-making between education, health and social care on the day after their 16th birthday.

> Sam's 16th birthday was 28 September. On 29 September, he attends a paediatrician appointment, where the doctor talks directly to him about a proposed course of medication. The paediatrician requires Sam's consent, not his parents. The paediatrician made the decision about

Sam's capacity to understand the treatment. At school, Sam joins the EHC Plan annual review meeting with his parents, which discusses possible post-16 options. Sam is asked for his views but, at this meeting, it is his parents who make the choices.

After the annual review meeting, Mr Khan, Sam's head of year, talks to Sam about participating in a sponsored walk for Children in Need. Mr Khan explains the arrangements for the walk, including enlisting sponsors and collecting the money after the walk. Sam decides he would like to take part. Mr Khan suggests Sam has a sixth form buddy to help him, Sam thinks this is a good idea, and agrees. Mr Khan reminds Sam to let his parents know he is taking part.

After school, Sam and his family meet the social worker to discuss the respite care arrangements. Sam's views are sought, but it is his parents who make the final decision.

Generally this book uses the term 'young person' with the same meaning as the Children and Families Act 2014 – a person who has completed Y11[2] but is under 25 years of age. Sometimes 'young person' will refer to the 16–25 age group, but this will be indicated. However, when the young person reaches their 18th birthday, in law, they are adults, and all adult legislation applies. Usually, in law, the term 'child' is used for someone under the age of 18.

Figures 1.1 to 1.3 show the legal frameworks that protect and support young people with SEN in educational settings up to the age of 25. Education professionals will be aware of their responsibilities in relation to educational, safeguarding and equality legislation.

---

2   The last Friday in June, provided the young person has reached their 16th birthday.

Introduction

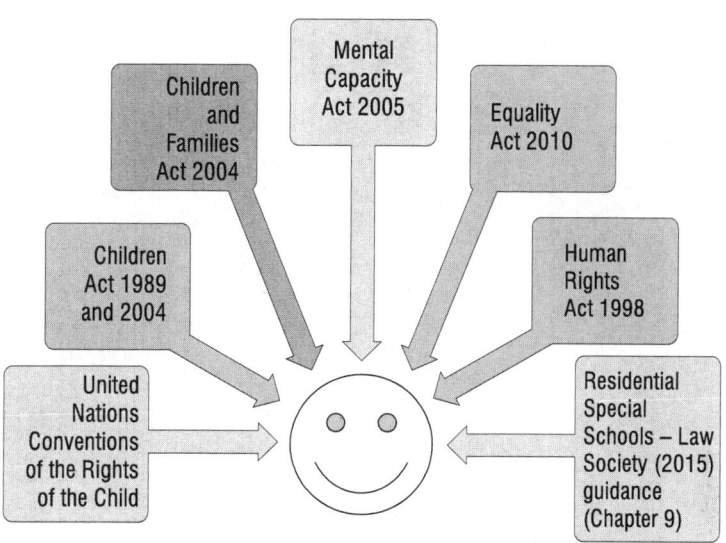

**Figure 1.1** Legal frameworks that protect and support young people aged 16–17 years 11 months with special educational needs in relation to receiving education in a school or further education setting

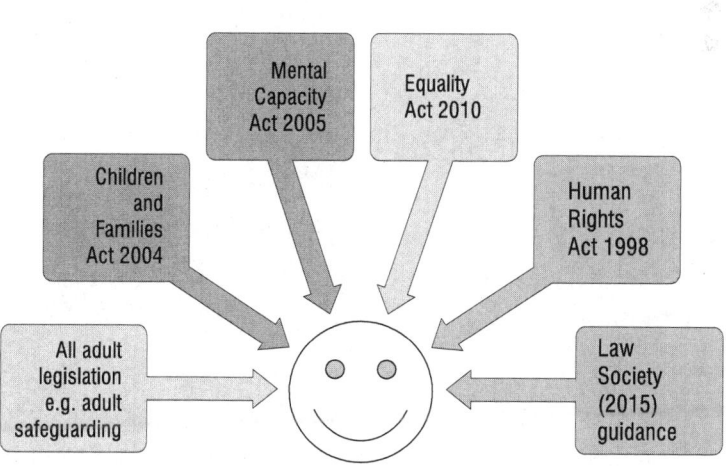

**Figure 1.2** Legal frameworks that protect and support 18–19-year-olds with special educational needs in relation to receiving education in a school settting

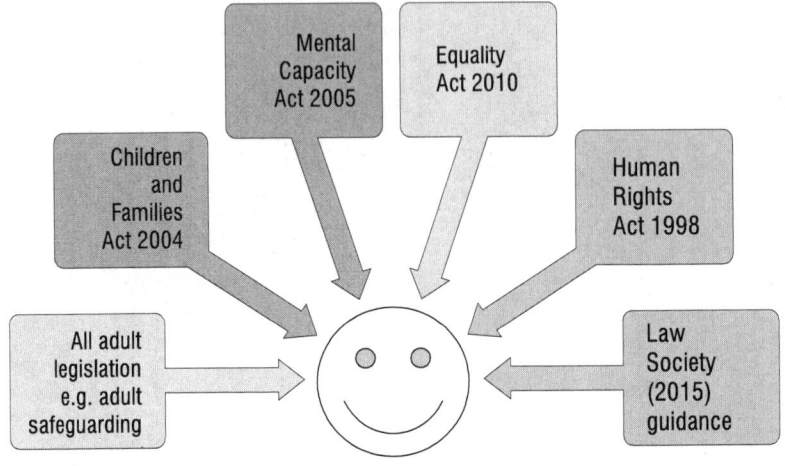

**Figure 1.3** Legal frameworks that protect and support 18–25-year-olds with special educational needs in relation to receiving education in a further education setting

## Summary

- The MCA applies from the age of 16.

- The MCA uses the term 'young person' to refer to someone aged 16–17.

- The Children and Families Act 2014 uses the term 'young person' to mean someone who has reached the end of Y11 (last Friday in June) and is under 25.

- The Children and Families Act 2014 gives young people the right to make decisions about the content of their EHC Plan from the end of Y11 (last Friday in June).

- For school activities that are not part of their special educational provision, a young person should be encouraged to make their own decisions from their 16th birthday.

- Young people receiving care and treatment from health professionals will be expected to make their own decisions about this from their 16th birthday.

- The Children Act 1989 underpins the way in which social workers work; this Act gives young people the right to make their own decisions at the age of 17.

- This book uses the term 'young person' to refer to someone in the 16–25 age range and to someone who has completed Y11 and is under 25; it will be indicated which age range is being used.

*Chapter 2*

# The MCA Five Principles

## Background

The Mental Capacity Act (MCA) 2005 and its Code of Practice (MCA COP) were formally introduced into education through the Children and Families Act 2014 and the accompanying *Special Educational Needs and Disability Code of Practice: 0–25 Years* (SEND COP). From 1 September 2014, all those working in education with the 16–25 age group *must* have regard to the SEND COP and *must also* have regard to the MCA COP. 'Must' here refers to a statutory requirement to follow the guidance in *both* codes of practice. Similar to the SEND COP, any departure from the MCA COP would require an explanation. *Reading this book is not a substitute for studying the MCA COP – at the very least Chapters 1–6, 12, 15 and 16 should be read.*

Like everyone who works with, or cares for, a young person who may lack capacity to make a particular decision, parents have to follow the MCA. Whilst parents do not have to follow the MCA COP in the same way as education professionals, they are advised to follow the guidance, as far as they are aware of it, as this will assist them in understanding and carrying out their duties under the MCA (MCA COP Introduction). The SEND COP Annex 1 notes that generally, when a young person lacks capacity, it is their parent(s) who will make the educational decision on their behalf. In this circumstance, parents should follow the MCA COP guidance about acting in a person's 'best interests' to ensure they act in their young person's 'best interests'.

There are two publications written for parents to help them understand the MCA and its role in education. These are the National Sensory Impairment Partnership (NatSIP) website document *No Decision About My Education Without Me. A Guide* for *Parents and Carers Helping Young People (16–25 years) Make their Own Decisions about their Education* (Sinson 2015) and the Preparing for Adulthood *Factsheet: The Mental Capacity Act 2005 and Supported Decision Making* (2015).

The MCA and its code of practice came into force in October 2007. Both are written in way that suggests they are predominantly aimed at people working in health and social care, and address some specific decisions in these areas. In 2007, the Department of Health supported the implementation of the MCA through a range of training materials and information. Since 2007 and until 1 September 2014, the main application of the MCA has been by health and social care professionals, although lawyers do use it.

An amendment to the MCA in 2009 introduced the Deprivation of Liberty Safeguards (DoLS), originally applying to adults in hospitals and registered care homes, and formed a supplement to the MCA COP. Following the March 2014 Supreme Court judgment, discussed below, the remit has been extended to all state-funded residential placements, including residential special schools and colleges. Despite references in the MCA COP (13.54) to an intention to revise the MCA COP to include DoLS, this has not happened, and it remains a separate document.

However, following the March 2014 Supreme Court judgement, the Law Commission has undertaken a consultation regarding new processes to replace the Deprivation of Liberty Safeguards. The consultation document concluded that the current system is 'deeply flawed' (Law Commission 2015)[1] and proposed a new system to be known as 'Protective Care', which focuses on providing appropriate care and better outcomes for people who lack capacity and helping their family and carers. It is proposed there will be a new Bill in 2016.

---

[1] www.lawcom.gov.uk/project/mental-capacity-and-deprivation-of-liberty.

## What is the Mental Capacity Act 2005?

> In this section 'young person' refers to the 16–25 age group. The terms 'mental capacity' and 'capacity' are used interchangeably to refer to a young person's mental capacity.

The MCA is a law covering England and Wales that gives everyone, from the age of 16, the right to make their own decisions (presumption of capacity). Most importantly, it provides a statutory framework to support and protect young people if they are unable to make a particular decision for themselves. It provides guidance on how to:

- support young people to make their own decisions as far as possible

- determine if a young person lacks capacity to make their own decision

- make a decision on behalf of a young person in their 'best interests'.

The MCA is founded on a 'functional approach' to the young person's ability to make a decision. This means that it is what the young person understands, or knows, or can do in relation to the particular decision that determines whether the young person can make this decision rather than the reason(s) for which they are considered to have special educational needs (SEN). Whilst education professionals will be very familiar with this approach, at the time the MCA was enacted, it was common for a judgement about a person's capacity to be based on their diagnosis.

The MCA COP (4.7) stipulates that a belief about a young person's capacity should not be based on their diagnosis, label, the way they look, the way they behave, or their age. For example, a young person with Down's syndrome cannot be assumed to lack capacity to make a particular decision because of the Down's syndrome. A functional approach recognises that there may be variability in a young person's ability to understand the relevant information, for example, due to its complexity or abstract nature, to make a specific decision, leading to each decision being considered individually. For instance, a young person may be able to choose what clothes to wear, but not understand the pertinent information to decide which college to attend. Therefore, the functional approach has no concept of 'general capacity' or 'general lack of capacity' – a young person's capacity needs to be considered for each decision.

The functional approach set out in the MCA COP fits with the SEND COP Assess, Plan, Do, Review (APDR) model. Both approaches are dynamic processes involving the modification, differentiation and adaptation of the information and resources to facilitate a young person's understanding. (See Chapter 4 for further discussion.)

## The Five Principles of the Mental Capacity Act 2005

The five principles, sometimes referred to as the statutory five principles, establish the core values of the MCA and are derived from human rights principles. These should underpin every action or decision concerning a young person's capacity to make a specific decision. Principles 1–3 are about enabling a young person's decision-making. Principles 4 and 5 guide those making decisions on behalf of a young person who lacks the capacity to make the particular decision. In relation to educational decisions, this will generally be the young person's parents (SEND COP Annex 1).

### *Principle 1: Presumption of capacity*

> It should be assumed a young person can make their own decisions unless it is proved they cannot do so.

This principle encapsulates two concepts – the presumption of capacity and the human rights principle of the right to autonomy. The presumption of capacity means that the starting point is *always* to assume that the young person *can* make the specific decision when it is needed. As noted above, a young person must not be considered to lack capacity because of their particular SEN, diagnosis, label, appearance or behaviour. However, factors relating to these may cause concern about the young person's ability to make the particular decision. In that case, those working with the young person should follow the guidance set out in the MCA COP Chapter 4, which is explained in this book, in Chapter 4.

The right to autonomy entitles the young person to make their own informed choices about their education. The young person's decision should be theirs and not due to coercion by others (MCA COP 2.8).

## Principle 2: Individuals being supported to make their own decisions

> A young person should have all the help and support possible to make and communicate their own decision before anyone decides that they lack the capacity to make their own decision.

In this principle, the emphasis on *'all the help and support possible'* should be noted. This refers to a young person being given all the information needed to make the decision in the format they best understand. Although this describes the way education professionals generally support young people, at the time the MCA was enacted, it was not a familiar approach for other professionals, for example, in health and social care. Chapter 3 of the MCA COP gives some guidance as to what 'all help and support possible' entails, including the use of visual aids, simplified language, assistive communication aids and breaking down information. Since it was written, however, there have been rapid advances in technology, for example, tablet computers that offer options for gathering and presenting the information.

> Jill is 17 years old with Down's syndrome and attends her local special school. She communicates using Makaton signing and saying some single words. She enjoys using

her iPad to take photos, play games and to assist her communication. In school and college, some lesson activities are also iPad-based.

Jill has to decide if she wants to remain in her current school for another year, or transfer to the local further education (FE) college for a life skills course. She has been attending the FE college for a day a week for the past year with other students and staff from her current school. In preparation for making the decision, the school staff have been talking with Jill, as well as assisting her to use her iPad to take photos of key staff and relevant places in college and school. School staff have used Jill's iPad to make some videos of her doing various activities in both settings. In addition, Jill has recorded her college tutor and school class teacher explaining and showing her what will be offered assuming she attends that educational establishment. This enables Jill to access the information when she wants to look at it. She is encouraged to show it to her parents so they can also talk to her about the choice she has to make.

## *Principle 3: Unwise decisions*

A young person should not be treated as lacking capacity just because they make an unwise decision.

Some health and social care organisations have amended this to include eccentric decisions: 'people have the right to make decisions that others might regard as unwise or eccentric' (SCIE website[2]).

This principle may present challenges and concerns to education professionals and parents. It is understandable to wish to protect young people from making what is felt to be the wrong choice, but the young person's choice should be respected if they have the capacity to make the decision.

---

2    Available at www.scie.org.uk/publications/mca/principles.asp.

Determining what constitutes an unwise or eccentric decision may be somewhat subjective. For example, the parent of a 17-year-old city dweller interested in falconry may believe their child is making an unwise decision to leave school to attend a college specialising in land industries rather than studying for more conventional qualifications. The parent of an 18-years-old young person with SEN may be concerned about the wisdom of their offspring's decision to leave education.

The Medical Protection Society offers guidance to doctors if they, or the young person's family, are concerned that the young person's decision puts them at risk of significant harm or exploitation, or seems to be out of character. It suggests consideration should be given to whether the choice fits with what is known about the young person's beliefs or values, and previous decisions or behaviours, in relation to this kind of issue.

Whilst this seems helpful and pragmatic advice, educationalists and parents are likely to be worried by the 23 October 2014 Court of Protection judgment in relation to a 22-year-old woman with a significant learning disability and functioning at the level of an immature 12–13-year-old. The young woman 'had a history of "abusive and exploitative relationships" with sexual partners' but on the evidence was considered to 'have the mental capacity to consent to sex' ([2014] EWCOP 38, reported in *The Independent* 25 October 2014). The judge acknowledged that he had misgivings about his judgment, but accepted the professional evidence indicated that the young woman met the legal capacity test; he did request the matter be kept under review. This reinforces that making risky choices is not indicative of a lack of capacity, and that young people are entitled to make such decisions.

In the scenario below, the young person makes an unexpected choice that, given her future aspirations and possibility of employment, both her tutor and parent consider to be unwise.

> Jill likes looking after animals. She has a cat, which she feeds daily, and helps her parents clean out the family's

hamster. Jill does not like seeing animals being hurt; she becomes upset if she sees animals on television being killed or having an operation.

At college, Jill has to choose between animal care and horticulture options with related work experience. Jill's Education, Health and Care (EHC) Plan aspiration section (Section A) notes that she wants to work with animals and that her aunt may let her 'work' at her cattery if Jill has received some training in animal care. Jill lives in a ground floor flat with no garden.

Mrs Jones, Jill's tutor, talks about the choices with Jill using photos, videos and visits to the potential work experience placements. When Jill has to make her decision, Mrs Jones explains and shows her all the information, including the video of her visiting the two work experience placements. Mrs Jones concludes that Jill demonstrated that she understood the information. Jill was able to say what she thought was good about each of the two choices; she genuinely seemed to like the idea of growing edible plants. To Mrs Jones' surprise, Jill picks the horticulture option; her knowledge of Jill suggested she would choose animal care. Nevertheless, Mrs Jones' assessment of Jill's capacity to make this decision concluded that, on the balance of probabilities, Jill has capacity. Mrs Jones, with Jill's permission, talks to Jill's mother about the decision. Jill's mother agrees it is an unexpected choice, and that it will affect whether Jill will be able to 'work' at her aunt's cattery.

The tutor's assessment is that Jill has the capacity to make the decision. Therefore, regardless of the possible consequences and views of others, the young person's choice is their decision.

## *Principle 4: 'Best interests'*

Actions or decisions carried out on behalf of a young person who lacks capacity must be in the young person's 'best interests'.

This principle, along with Principle 5, is guidance for those making decisions on behalf of a young person who lacks capacity. In relation to decisions about a young person's education, as noted above, the SEND COP Annex 1 states this will generally be the parents of the young person. Anyone, including parents, making a decision on behalf of a young person who lacks capacity should follow the 'best interests' checklist set out in the MCA COP Chapter 5, and discussed in this book's Chapter 8.

The SEND COP (8.16) lists the decisions the young person has the right to make in relation to their SEN and special educational provision. Nonetheless, as young people are part of a school or college community, there are likely to be other choices that are unrelated to special educational provision, such as participating in a school or college event, which are outside the remit of the SEND COP. It can be reasonably assumed that a young person's parents will also make these decisions if the young person lacks the capacity to do so.

## *Principle 5: Less restrictive option*

> Actions or decisions carried out on behalf of a young person who lacks capacity should limit their rights and freedoms as little as possible.

This MCA principle provides guidance to those making decisions on behalf of a young person who lacks capacity to make the particular decision. Nevertheless, the starting point is ensuring that young people are enabled to make those choices where they are able to do so. This may be everyday decisions, such as what to wear, what to eat and what to do in the lunch break. It is important that outcomes and steps written into an EHC Plan support the young person making their own choices, as far as possible, and develop their independence.

The concept of restricting freedom is on a continuum; at one end is total freedom regardless of any limits, and at the other, depriving someone of their liberty. Somewhere between the continuum's midpoint and deprivation of liberty end sits the notion of restriction of liberty. As noted above, the MCA covers this in the DoLS supplement. This applies to state-funded residential settings, which include residential special schools, residential special colleges (18+), foster placements and supported living in the community.

The Children and Families Act 2014 covers more than just special educational needs, which are set out in Part 3. Part 5 (Welfare of Children) introduces 'staying put arrangements' that allow a young person to remain in foster care until the age of 21 rather than 18. Local authorities offer supported living schemes that enable adults to live independently in their own home, so some young people attending day educational placements may be living in foster care or supported living. Thus, *all* education professionals need an awareness of DoLS as it can be considered part of their safeguarding responsibilities.

The Law Society (2015) guidance, commissioned by the Department of Health, following the Supreme Court judgment discussed below, provides thought-provoking information about restriction and deprivation of liberty, which is *very relevant* to education professionals. The guidance covers a range of residential settings including residential special schools, foster homes, supported living and respite care, as well as a chapter specifically addressing the issue in relation to those aged 16–17.

### Deprivation of liberty

In March 2014 the Supreme Court gave a new definition to what is meant by 'deprivation of liberty' ([2014] UKSC 19). This has become known as the 'acid test', and is used by local authorities to determine whether restrictions amount to a deprivation of liberty.

Deprivation of liberty is as follows:

> The young person is under continuous supervision and control *and* is not free to leave *and* the young person lacks capacity to consent to these arrangements.

All three conditions have to apply:

- 'Continuous supervision and control' means that those caring for the young person in the residential setting 'exercise complete and effective control of the young person's care and movements' ([2014] UKSC 19). That is, care staff, foster parents or support workers make all the choices for the young person, such as where they can go, who they see, whom they can contact and what they do. The young person is not able to do any of the things they wish to do.
- 'Free to leave' means that the young person is able to leave the school, college, foster home or supported living and live where they choose.

For young people aged 16–17 the Supreme Court added additional criteria for determining deprivation of liberty – this age group should be compared to other young people of a similar age and maturity without disabilities. The Law Society (2015) explains that this means the starting point is to consider how different the care arrangements are for a particular young person with SEN or a disability from those that would generally be made for someone of the same age and relative maturity who do not have SEN or a disability. If the arrangements are the usual limitations that would be in place for this age group and level of maturity, then there is no restriction or deprivation of liberty. For example, a residential school may have a rule that when out shopping young people aged 16–17 cannot spend their pocket money on cigarettes or alcohol. This is usual, as it is illegal for young people of this age to do so. On the other hand, if the care arrangements for a 16-year-old with SEN involve the same level of constraints that would be in place for the average five-year-old, then it should be considered that this may be a restriction or deprivation of liberty. This considers the actual matter of whether the young person is deprived of their liberty or it is restricted; it does not address whether this is in the young person's best interests, which it may be.

The Law Society (2015) guidance suggests that looking at a young person's whole care plan, including the EHC Plan, rather than individual elements, may be a better guide to whether the arrangements constitute a restriction or deprivation of liberty.

The difference between a restriction or deprivation of liberty is a matter of intensity and degree, and not nature. It will depend on how much greater the intensity of supervision, support and restrictions are than would usually apply to someone of that age and maturity without disabilities. That is, how much, how often and for how long. There is no consensus on what time period is considered too long and therefore a deprivation of liberty. For example, managing a young person's (aged 16–25) challenging behaviour by the frequent use of seclusion that they are not free to leave, for long periods of time, is likely to be considered a deprivation of liberty. Occasionally a short time in seclusion, alongside a range of techniques for managing the young person's challenging behaviour, may be considered a restriction rather than deprivation of liberty.

The Law Society (2015) acknowledges that there is uncertainty about what level of constraints are usually applied to all 16-year-olds without SEN or disabilities. It does state that it is generally expected, that, as young people approach adulthood, the intensity and degree of restrictions reduce as they mature and become independent.

Parents cannot authorise arrangements for their young person that are a deprivation of liberty; only the Court of Protection can do this. Parents can sanction arrangements that amount to a restriction of liberty, but consideration should be given to whether it is in the young person's best interests.

Residential colleges (18+) also must apply to the Court of Protection if arrangements they wish to put in place deprive a young person of their liberty.

### Implications for educational settings

In reality, everyone has some level of restriction placed on their freedom to do exactly as they please, whether this is by an employer, family or society more generally. Educational establishments have regulations relating to their ability to restrict the freedoms of young people educated therein. Whilst generally the use of physical restraint may be considered as a liberty-restricting measure, schools are permitted to use proportionate restraint to prevent a pupil committing an offence, causing personal injury or damage to property, or behaviour that affects the good order or discipline being maintained (Law Society 2015). Equally, a young person who lacks capacity to consent to a specific educational placement, particularly a residential one, cannot be considered to have been deprived of their liberty, although measures put in place by the establishment may do so.

Although the notion of deprivation of liberty applies to residential settings, for example, the residential part of a residential special school or college, the pertinent issue that contributed to the Supreme Court judgment, carers making decisions on behalf of the vulnerable young people, can be extrapolated into the classroom, be it a residential or non-residential educational establishment. This has implications for the way in which young people are supported by educational establishment staff to fulfil the aims of the Children and Families Act 2014 of involving young people, as far as possible, in decisions about their education, developing their independence and preparation for adulthood.

The school or college day is divided into lesson and break times. During break times, young people should be given options about what they can do, for example, go to the canteen, attend a club, listen to music, and be helped to make a choice. Within lessons, a young person should be supported to do things for themselves, even if this means the task is not completed but what was achieved was done by the young person. Consider these scenarios:

> Jill attends the local FE college and is following a life skills course. She is in a practical session to make a ham, cheese or ham and cheese sandwich with white or brown bread. The students choose which sandwich to prepare and follow the instructions presented in a sequence of photographs. The task entails getting all the ingredients from the fridge, finding a plate and knife and then making

the sandwich. Jill tends to work slowly but can achieve the outcome. There are five students in the kitchen area with a tutor and two learning assistants (Mrs Darcy and Ms Bingley).

Scenario 1: Jill looks at the first photo, showing the ham, cheese and margarine in the fridge, for a long time. Mrs Darcy gets the ham and margarine from the fridge for Jill and gives her two slices of white bread. She gives Jill the second photo and shows her where the knife and plate are kept. Mrs Darcy stays by Jill's place whilst she gets these. Mrs Darcy remains at Jill's side whilst she looks at the third picture showing margarine being spread on the bread. Jill pauses; Mrs Darcy takes the lid off the margarine and gives Jill the knife. Jill spreads the margarine on the bread and pauses again. Mrs Darcy gives Jill the ham to put on the bread, which she does. Mrs Darcy puts the second slice of bread on top and cuts the sandwich in half for Jill.

Scenario 2: Jill looks at the first photo, showing the ham, cheese and margarine in the fridge, for a long time. Ms Bingley asks Jill which sandwich she wants to make, Jill points to the cheese in the photo. Ms Bingley shows Jill the white and brown bread and asks her to choose which she wants; Jill chooses the brown. Ms Bingley moves on to another student and Jill goes to the fridge for the cheese and margarine. On returning to her place, she looks at the second photo. After a few minutes, Jill goes to the cupboard, takes a plate and collects a knife from the cutlery box. As she looks at the third photo showing margarine being spread on the bread, Ms Bingley returns and asks Jill if she wants margarine on her bread, Jill nods, picks up the knife and slowly spreads margarine on both slices of bread. She pauses before putting the cheese on one slice of the bread followed by the second slice of bread. Ms Bingley returns to see how Jill is progressing; seeing the finished sandwich she asks Jill if she wants to cut the sandwich into two or four pieces. Ms Bingley shows Jill the photo of sandwiches cut in half or quarters. Jill points to the quarters and then to Ms Bingley, which Ms Bingley interprets as Jill wishing her to cut the sandwich, possibly because Jill is unsure how to cut it into four pieces. Ms Bingley demonstrates how to cut it, and traces marks with the knife on the sandwich so Jill can do it.

In scenario 1, the learning assistant made all the choices for Jill, and provided a high level of supervision that did not allow Jill to complete the task herself. Therefore, the model of support in Scenario 1 can be considered to restrict Jill's rights and freedoms within the context of the lesson. Scenario 2 provided a model of support that enabled Jill to make her own decisions and complete the task herself with an appropriate level of supervision.

### Residential schools

Residential school staff should familiarise themselves with the Law Society (2015) guidance in terms of developing policy, procedure and practice, and understanding measures that are considered to be restrictions of liberty. The Law Society presents a set of considerations for professionals that would make a good starting point for discussion. The guidance may present challenges as schools have to meet the needs of young people with a wide range of differing needs.

## The Mental Capacity Act 2005 Code of Practice

The SEND COP and MCA COP both set out the way their respective laws works in practice and are guidance that should be followed; the SEND COP includes the MCA COP. Both note who or which roles should have regard to the respective codes of practice. The MCA COP documents the responsibilities for frontline workers in health and social care, presuming that all have the necessary training or experience to follow the requirements. The SEND COP is more wide-ranging, detailing the duties and responsibilities for frontline workers, as well as administrators in education, health and social care. Incorporating the MCA COP into the SEND COP raises the prospect that not everyone who has to have regard to the MCA COP is trained, or experienced, in working directly with young people with SEN. This may particularly relate to local authority officers who maintain EHC Plans or manage applications for personal budgets. There may be circumstances when it is necessary for these officers to assess a young person's capacity to consider amendments to their EHC Plan or a personal budget request. The MCA COP does permit someone assessing a young person's capacity to seek assistance from another professional to advise.

The MCA COP differs from the SEND COP as it was written with health and social care professionals in mind rather than people working in education. This is reflected in both the language used to describe a person's functioning and the scenarios provided to illustrate points – adult health and social care issues. Although the MCA has provisions for the government to revise the MCA COP, it has not been amended in any way since it was first published in 2007, nor are there plans to do so; the DoLS, added in 2009, remain a supplement. Consequently, the MCA COP may present some challenges for both education professionals and parents.

Educationalists will find terms such as 'impairment of mind or brain' and 'disturbance in the functioning of the mind or brain' very alien and not in keeping with the functional approach to ability promoted in education. This terminology forms the basis of the criteria to consider whether a young person may lack capacity to make a specific decision, possibly leading to a formal assessment of their capacity to do so. Therefore, the prominence given to these terms in the MCA and MCA COP means that, however uncomfortable educationalists feel using them, they cannot be ignored or glossed over. Nonetheless, this terminology is difficult to equate with a strengths and difficulties/weakness-based description of functioning. Hence, this wording must be translated into more accessible concepts to enable consideration of those who may meet the criteria to possibly lack capacity to make a specific decision. Although the SEND COP offers no interpretation of these terms for education professionals, the Department for Education (2014,

Annex A) and Department of Health (2015, Chapter 2) do give insight into what is meant by them.

The MCA COP introduces roles that may be unfamiliar to educationalists such as Independent Mental Capacity Advocates (IMCAs) and deputies appointed by the Court of Protection. However, education professionals will probably rarely encounter these roles. A young person will be allocated an IMCA if they lack capacity to make a decision about serious medical treatment and they do not have any family or a friend who can make the decision on their behalf. Deputies are appointed by the Court of Protection to manage the property and financial affairs, or the health and welfare, of someone who lacks the capacity to do so themselves. If the young person's only income is from state benefits, an appointee manages this if the young person lacks capacity to manage their finances. Appointees can be family members, friends or professionals, such as solicitors, but the person has to be approved by the Department for Works and Pensions (DWP).

## *Court of Protection*

Education professionals are familiar with the First-tier SEN and Disability (SEND) Tribunal for resolving differences of opinion between a parent and local authority in matters relating to a statement of SEN, which, under the Children and Families Act 2014, is known as an Education, Health and Care (EHC) Plan. Parents or a young person (after the end of Y11 – last Friday in June) can appeal to the SEND Tribunal to resolve the disputes relating to an EHC Plan set out in the SEND COP (11.45). Chapter 5 of this book discusses a young person's capacity to appeal to the SEND Tribunal; in legal jargon, this is termed as 'to bring an appeal'.

The Court of Protection (the Court) is a specialist court, with the same status as the High Court, established under the MCA to oversee actions under this legislation. The Court of Protection's function is to protect individuals who lack the capacity to make a specific decision themselves and to make decisions in the person's 'best interests'. Within an educational context, the most likely issues will relate to a young person's capacity to make a decision and 'best interests' decisions made on their behalf when they lack capacity to make a particular decision. The Court also follows the MCA five principles in order to make its decisions. Like the SEND Tribunal, the Court is the last resort when the dispute resolution processes, set out in the MCA COP, have not enabled agreement about a young person's capacity or 'best interests' decisions made on their behalf. However, if a specialist residential college, foster home or supported living scheme wishes to institute restrictions on the young person that amount to a deprivation of liberty, the establishment *must* make an application to the Court of Protection for permission.

So, is it envisaged that education professionals will make applications to the Court of Protection, or is it more likely to be the parents? This will depend on who disagrees with whom about what. As noted above, a parent or young person disagreeing with the local authority about the content of an EHC Plan will still appeal to the SEND Tribunal. Differences of opinion relating to a belief about a young person's capacity to make a specific decision, or whether a young person's parent is acting in their 'best interests', are matters that could ultimately be referred to the Court of Protection.

> Jill is 18 years old with Down's syndrome and attends the local FE college. She communicates using Makaton signing and saying some single words. She enjoys using her iPad to take photos, play games and to assist her communication. Jill likes looking after animals. She has a cat, which she feeds daily, and helps her parents clean out the family's hamster.
>
> Jill is following a life skills course and has to choose between animal care and horticulture options with related work experience. Jill's EHC Plan aspiration section (Section A) notes that she wants to work with animals and that her aunt may let her 'work' in her cattery if Jill has received some training in animal care. Jill lives in a ground floor flat with no garden.

Mrs Jones, Jill's tutor, talks about the choices to Jill using photos, videos and visits to the potential work experience placements. When Jill has to make her decision, Mrs Jones explains and shows her all the information, including the video of her visiting the two work experience placements. Mrs Jones concludes that Jill demonstrated that she understood the information. Jill was able to say what she thought was good about each of the two choices; she genuinely seemed to like the idea of growing edible plants. To Mrs Jones' surprise, Jill picks the horticulture option; her knowledge of Jill suggested she would choose animal care. Nevertheless, Mrs Jones' assessment of Jill's capacity to make this decision concluded that, on the balance of probabilities, Jill has capacity. Mrs Jones, with Jill's permission, talks to Jill's mother about the decision. Jill's mother (Mrs Walsh) agrees it is an unexpected choice and questions Jill's capacity to make the decision. Mrs Walsh states she wants Jill to take the animal care option, as it would provide the experience Jill's aunt requires to let Jill help at her cattery. Mrs Jones reminds Jill's mother that the capacity assessment indicated that Jill has the capacity to make the choice.

Mrs Jones explains to Jill's mother that the college has good links with the council's Parks and Gardens department where young people have been offered regular opportunities when they have completed the horticulture option. In addition, some garden centres have a similar arrangement.

As there is disagreement about Jill's capacity to make this decision, Mrs Jones invites Jill's mother to a formal meeting to discuss Jill's capacity assessment for this decision. Mrs Jones arranges for another tutor (Ms Robinson), who knows Jill well, to undertake another capacity assessment for the option choices. Ms Robinson also concludes that Jill has capacity to make the choice; she chose the horticulture option again. Mrs Walsh is not convinced by either tutor that Jill has the capacity to make the decision. As the choice has a bearing on the future options available to Jill, Mrs Walsh makes an application to the Court of Protection to determine Jill's capacity for this decision.

In the discussion of Principle 3 above, there is reference to a Court of Protection case ([2014] EWCOP 38) that was reported in both broadsheet and tabloid newspapers. Education professionals and parents may be very concerned that cases before this court can be reported in the media, although Court of Protection appeals are heard in private – the press can attend, but the public cannot. However, what journalists are permitted to report is very strictly controlled. Some types of cases can always be reported, such as those involving applications for deprivation of liberty, but journalists must adhere to the regulations. Other cases can only be reported if the judge hearing the appeal gives permission. In all cases, the subject of the application, their family and friends, are anonymous. In the case discussed in 'unwise decisions' above ([2014] EWCOP 38), the judge stated that the woman with learning disabilities was to be referred to as AC, her father EC, her mother LC and the social worker DT in the judgment. Expert witnesses and public bodies, but not individual employees, are named unless there is a compelling reason not to do so. In this case, most newspapers did not use 'AC' but referred to her as 'the woman'; the social worker was referred to by her job title; and some newspapers named the local authority.

## Summary

- The MCA and its accompanying COP have been introduced into education through the Children and Families Act 2014. The MCA:
    - applies from 16 years old and gives young people the right to make their own decisions, as well as providing a framework to support and protect young people who lack the capacity to make a particular decision

- is based on a functional approach to a young person's decision-making
- has five principles that underpin every action or decision about a young person's capacity to make a particular decision
- has a primary principle of the presumption of capacity
- established the Court of Protection to oversee actions under this legislation
- has a code of practice (MCA COP) that sets out how the law works in practice.

- The MCA COP:
  - presumes either training or experience of working with people who may lack capacity to make decisions. This may not be the case for all education professionals who have to have regard to the MCA COP
  - was predominantly written for health and social care professional, so some language and examples used to illustrate matters will be unfamiliar to educationalists
  - DoLS are a supplement to the MCA COP and remain a separate document. DoLS apply to residential colleges (18+), foster homes, supported living in the community and respite care.

- Education professionals working with the 16–25 age group *must* have regard to both the SEND COP *and* MCA COP.

- Parents are advised to follow the MCA COP when they are making decisions on behalf of their young person who lacks capacity to make a specific decision.

*Chapter 3*

# Mental Capacity and to Lack Capacity

> **Recap**
> - The Mental Capacity Act (MCA) 2005 takes a functional approach to capacity.
> - Beliefs about a young person's capacity should not be based on their special educational needs, diagnosis, label, the way they look or behave or their age.
> - The terms 'mental capacity' and 'capacity' are used interchangeably to refer to a young person's mental capacity.
> - Not all young people receiving support under the SEND COP will meet the MCA COP criteria for it to be considered they may lack capacity to make a particular decision.
> - MCA COP – Mental Capacity Act 2005 Code of Practice.

## Mental capacity

Mental capacity means the ability to make a decision – any decision. The MCA defines the ability to make a decision as comprising of four components, *all* of which have to be achieved for the young person to be considered to have capacity. The components are to:

- understand the information relevant to the decision
- retain the information long enough to make the decision
- use and weigh the information to arrive at a choice
- communicate the decision in any way.

The MCA has no notion of partial capacity; the young person either does, or does not, meet the criteria. From an educationalist's perspective, this requirement may seem harsh and out of step with the Children and Families Act 2014 core principle of young people being involved in decision-making as fully as possible. However, the MCA has an inbuilt safeguard in the 'best interests' checklist and associated guidance (MCA COP Chapter 5) to ensure the young person's views, wishes and feelings are considered by the person making the decision on behalf of a young person who lacks capacity to do so. Nevertheless, education professionals may still find this blunt approach discomfiting. Focusing on positives, the MCA emphasises that a young person's capacity must be considered for each decision; as noted in Chapter 2, there is no concept of 'general capacity', and nor is it regarded as static. Thus, a young person may be able to choose which college to attend, but not understand the support they will need. Whilst young people remain in education there is the opportunity to try to improve and extend their decision-making ability. Consideration could be given to including decision-making as an Education, Health and Care (EHC) Plan outcome. This aligns with the SEND COP emphasis on preparation for adulthood and independent living (SEND COP Chapter 8).

## *Types of decisions*

The MCA COP (4.1) classifies decisions as:

A  *Decisions about everyday life*, such as what to wear, what to eat or drink, what to do at lunchtime, where to sit, who to sit next to, which computer game to play, which magazine to look at, which task to do first, or whether to join a college outing.

Although this sort of decision does not require any formal assessment of the young person's decision-making capacity, it is important that those working with young people ensure they uphold the MCA principle of the presumption of capacity and the associated right to autonomy. The significance of young people being enabled to make choices for themselves is highlighted in the

Supreme Court judgment [2014] UKSC 19, discussed in Chapter 2. Whilst the concept of 'deprivation of liberty' is not applicable to day educational establishments, the contributory factors identified, that constitute a deprivation of liberty, are relevant considerations to anyone working with young people, the key issue being that those caring for vulnerable adults made all the decisions on their behalf.

B  *Decisions the MCA COP refers to as 'more serious or significant',* such as which college to choose, whether to move to a different educational establishment, how to travel to college, what support is needed, which course to study, choosing EHC Plan outcomes, or selecting a work experience placement.

C  *Decisions that may have 'legal consequences'* such as contracts or engaging in court procedures. In relation to education, this would include the young person asking the local authority for a personal budget or appealing to the First-tier SEND Tribunal about the content of their EHC Plan.

The decisions described in B and C may require a formal assessment of a young person's capacity to make a particular decision. In an educational context, 'more serious or significant decisions' seems vague. Within health and social care, this refers to decisions that have long-term or life-changing consequences, such as moving accommodation, having surgery or other medical treatment. This suggests that any decisions about the content of or amendments to a young person's EHC Plan are 'more serious or significant decisions', as the effects of these decisions have a lifespan of at least a year.

As discussed in Chapter 1, educational establishments generally offer more than the academic curriculum – there are social events, as well as extracurricular activities. Is the young person's decision to participate in one of these an everyday decision or a 'more serious and significant decision'? Inferring from the factors noted above, risk would seem to be a factor in decisions categorised as 'more serious and significant'. Consider these two scenarios:

> Sam is 19 years and attends the local further education (FE) college; he is following a life skills course. He is the subject of an EHC Plan due to learning difficulties.
>
> Scenario A: Mr Khan, Sam's tutor, talks to Sam about taking part in the life skills department's voluntary sponsored walk for Children in Need during the college day. The route involves circuits around the nearby park. Staff will be joining the students on the walk. Mr Khan explains the arrangements for the walk including signing up sponsors, and collecting the money afterwards. Mr Khan reassures Sam that he will have help from staff to enlist sponsors and collect the money. Sam decides he would like to take part.
>
> Scenario B: Mr Khan, Sam's tutor, talks to Sam about taking part in the life skills department's rock climbing and abseiling activities at an outdoor education centre. Mr Khan explains what is involved, and that, although safety equipment is used, there are risks. Sam decides he would like to take part.

Participating in the sponsored walk is a short-term activity and there would seem to be minimal risks, so perhaps Sam's decision to join the activity could be considered an 'everyday decision'. Nonetheless, the level of risk posed by any particular activity may be linked to the specific needs of the young person. For some young people a risk assessment may be appropriate and the outcome may help determine if the decision to take part is a 'more serious or significant' one. Scenario B, although a short-term activity, entails risks, and therefore Sam's participation could be regarded as a 'more serious or significant decision'.

## To lack capacity

A young person will be considered to 'lack capacity' if they have an impairment or disturbance that affects the way their mind or brain works, *and* the impairment or disturbance affects their ability to make specific decision at the time it needs to be made (MCA COP 4.3).

Functionally, it means that the young person was *not able* to do one or more of the following:

- understand the information relevant to the decision
- retain the information long enough to make the decision
- use and weigh the information to arrive at a choice
- communicate their decision in any way.

A young person's capacity to make a particular decision may have to be established through a formal capacity assessment as set out in the MCA COP Chapter 4 and discussed in this book, in Chapter 4.

As noted above, each decision should be considered individually, and those working with young people must ensure they adhere to the MCA principles. Young people should be given all the assistance possible to enable their decision-making, before it can be concluded that they lack capacity to do so. This does not mean asking the young person if they wish to make the decision or whether their parents should do so on their behalf. For some decisions, and/or for some young people, giving all the help possible may be a time-consuming process, but it is necessary to ensure that the young person is afforded the opportunity to make their own choice. The onus is on the person who needs the young person to make the particular decision to ensure sufficient time is allocated to the young person and their decision.

The MCA COP (4.10) states that anyone claiming a young person lacks capacity to make a particular decision when it is needed should be able to provide proof that, on the balance of probabilities, this is the case.

## Capacity, and Education, Health and Care Plans

- Being the subject of an EHC Plan has no bearing on a young person's capacity to make a particular decision when it is needed.

- A young person's capacity status cannot be written into an EHC Plan, as this has to be determined for each decision. There is no such thing as 'general capacity'. Taking a functional approach to capacity acknowledges that a young person's decision-making ability may vary in relation to the nature and complexity of the decision. Thus, a young person may be able to choose options within a course, but not which college to attend.

- It is not an indicator of a lack of capacity if, for example, when choosing post-16 options, the young person decides they wish to do something different from the post-16 plan that has been discussed by their parents, and educational professionals, since Year 9 (Y9).

## Summary

- Mental capacity is the ability to make a decision – any decision.

- The ability to make a decision has four components that *all* have to be achieved for the young person to be considered to have capacity to make the particular decision.

- To lack capacity means:
    o the young person has an impairment or disturbance that affects the way the mind or brain works
    o this affects the young person's ability to make a particular decision when it needs to be made
    o functionally the young person is unable to achieve one or more of the four decision-making components.

- Being the subject of an EHC Plan has no bearing on a young person's capacity to make a particular decision at the time it is needed.

- The MCA COP classifies decisions as 'everyday', 'more serious or significant' and those with 'legal consequences'.

- Not all young people receiving support under the SEND COP will meet the MCA COP criteria for it to be considered that they may lack capacity to make a particular decision.

- A formal capacity assessment may be required to establish a young person's ability to make a 'more serious or significant' or 'legal consequences' decision.

- A young person cannot be considered to lack capacity to make the particular decision unless they have been given all the help and support possible to do so. This may be a time-consuming process.

- Capacity status cannot be written into an EHC Plan, as a young person's ability to make a 'more serious or significant decision' or 'legal consequences' decision must be ascertained for each decision.

# Part 2

# Assessing a Young Person's Mental Capacity

*Chapter 4*

# 'More Serious or Significant Decisions'

> **Note**
> - In this chapter, 'young person' refers to the 16–25 age group.
> - The terms 'mental capacity' and 'capacity' are used interchangeably to refer to a young person's mental capacity.
> - SEND COP – *Special Educational Needs and Disability Code of Practice: 0–25 years.*
> - MCA COP – Mental Capacity Act 2005 Code of Practice.
> - Reading the MCA COP is strongly recommended – Chapters 2, 3 and 4 provide guidance about capacity assessments and supporting young people to make their own decisions.

An assessment of a young person's capacity to make a particular decision is founded in the Mental Capacity Act (MCA) 2005 principles and concepts discussed in previous chapters. To recap:

- Principle 1 of the MCA is the presumption of capacity.

- Principle 2 states that a young person should be given all the help and support possible to enable them to make and communicate their own decision.

- The MCA is founded on a functional approach to capacity.

- A young person's capacity to make a particular decision is determined for each decision.

- A judgement about a young person's capacity should not be based on their special educational needs (SEN), diagnosis, label, appearance, behaviour or age.

- Not all young people receiving support under the SEND COP, or who are the subject of an EHC Plan, will meet the criteria for it to be considered they may lack capacity to make a particular decision.

## What is a capacity assessment?

The SEND COP Annex 1 provides brief, and inaccurate, information about capacity assessments. Despite the DfE being informed of the shortcomings in Annex 1, it made no amendments to it for the re-publication of the SEND COP in January 2015. Therefore, this section remains flawed and misleading. It is very important that the correct procedure for undertaking a capacity assessment, as described in the MCA COP Chapter 4 and explained below, is followed.

A capacity assessment is a two-stage process that answers two questions that are set out in the MCA and the MCA COP Chapter 4. The Stage 1 question establishes whether the young person meets the criteria for it to be considered that they may lack capacity to make this decision. If the young person *does not* meet these criteria, then it *cannot be considered* that they may lack capacity (MCA COP 4.11), and therefore it *must* be assumed the young person has capacity to make this decision. This has been omitted from the SEND COP Annex 1, and has led to misunderstandings, for example, education professionals believing that all young people with an Education, Health and Care (EHC) Plan need to have their capacity assessed. It would be inappropriate to undertake a capacity assessment of young person who does not meet the criteria.

If the young person meets the Stage 1 criteria, then consideration is given to the Stage 2 question. This is answered using, what the SEND COP Annex 1 calls, the 'four key questions', and determines whether the young person has, or lacks, capacity to make this particular decision. The phrase 'four key questions' has been coined by the SEND COP Annex 1's authors; it is not terminology used in the MCA or MCA COP. Nevertheless, it is a useful way of referring to the elements of a capacity assessment.

The 'four key questions' form the basis of a capacity assessment and are reproduced in the SEND COP Annex 1 from the MCA and MCA COP, but not the actual Stage 2 question. As noted in Chapter 2, the wording used in these questions will seem alien, but the author suggests a translation into more familiar concepts. Nonetheless, it is advised that the original wording from the MCA COP is always included, as this is the legal wording. The author's interpretation would have no standing if the outcome of a capacity assessment was challenged either in the Court of Protection or in a First-tier Tribunal (SEND) hearing.

The MCA COP describes the outcome of a capacity assessment as either being 'on the balance of probabilities' (4.10) or a 'reasonable belief' (4.44) that the young person has, or lacks, capacity. These are not interchangeable phrases; professionals, having undertaken a formal capacity assessment, should describe the outcome as being 'on the balance of probabilities', whereas carers, who do not have to be specialists in assessing capacity, are advised to use the phrase 'reasonable belief' to describe their judgement about a young person's capacity (4.44). In the case studies presented in previous chapters, where a formal capacity assessment has been undertaken by an education professional, the phrase 'on the balance of probabilities' is used to describe the outcome.

## Capacity assessment questions
### Stage 1 question

- MCA COP (4.11): Does the young person have an impairment of, or a disturbance in the functioning of, their mind or brain?

- Author's interpretation: Does the young person have learning difficulties or learning disability, or difficulties with their emotional wellbeing or mental health issues?

## Stage 2 question

- MCA COP (4.13): Does the impairment or disturbance mean that the young person is unable to make a specific decision when they need to?

- Author's interpretation: Does the young person's learning difficulty or learning disability, emotional wellbeing difficulties or mental health issues mean that the young person is unable to make a specific decision when they need to?

## Formulating an interpretation understandable to education professionals

Analysing the MCA COP wording is akin to assembling a jigsaw puzzle, with scattered pieces, to formulate a sensible interpretation, couched in terms and concepts comprehended by education professionals. The starting point is the MCA COP (4.12) examples of what may constitute an 'impairment of or disturbance in' the functioning of the brain or mind. These are mainly diagnoses or labels such as 'conditions associated with some forms of mental illness' (p.44), dementia, symptoms of alcohol or drug abuse, rather than describing aspects of functioning. Whilst it does include significant learning disabilities, the other labels or diagnoses may be less familiar and not commonly associated with young people. Overall, this list seems to contradict the functional approach embedded in the MCA. However, the Stage 2 question returns to the MCA emphasis on functioning, regardless of label or diagnosis. Implicitly, this suggests it is likely only to be a small proportion of people who have an impairment in, or disturbance of, the functioning of their mind or brain, who may lack capacity to make a particular decision. Applying this to young people receiving support under the SEND COP suggests that it will probably be a small subset of this population who may lack capacity to make the specific decision. The challenge is to understand which young people may meet the Stage 1 question criteria to be considered to possibly lack capacity to make a particular decision. The SEND COP itself offers no guidance on this matter, and refers the reader to the MCA COP. So the quest continues.

Broadly, the Stage 1 and 2 questions can be reasonably interpreted as referring to learning difficulties or disabilities, mental health and emotional wellbeing issues.

### Learning difficulties and learning disabilities

This is another area where the MCA COP and SEND COP language differs. The MCA COP (4.12) refers to 'significant learning disabilities', terminology favoured by health and social care professionals. Learning disabilities are defined in the diagnostic manuals (for example, the International Classification of Diseases-10 (ICD10)) used by healthcare professionals. These definitions all include three components – significantly impaired intelligence, impaired social and adaptive functioning – that developed before adulthood. In keeping with a functional approach, the Department of Health (2001) redefined this as, 'a significantly reduced ability to understand new or complex information, or to learn new skills (impaired intelligence), with a reduced ability to cope independently (impaired social functioning), which started before adulthood, with a lasting effect on development' (p.14). This was intended to encompass people with a broad range of difficulties, but specifically notes that it does not include all those who are deemed to have learning difficulties under the educational definition of this term. It encourages consideration and assessment of a person's social functioning and communication skills.

Historically within education, there has been a difference in language between compulsory and post-16 education. School-based education professionals used the term 'learning difficulties', whereas post-16 staff referred to 'learning difficulties and disabilities' (LDD). The SEND COP (Introduction xvii) acknowledges this, and indicates that the umbrella term 'special educational needs' includes LDD. The post-16 Learning Difficulty Assessment definition of a learning difficulty (DfE 2013) is the same as the SEND COP (Introduction xiv) 'learning difficulty' – 'significantly greater difficulty learning than the majority of others of the same age'. LDD had a wide definition including young people with mental health problems, autistic spectrum conditions, attention deficit hyperactivity disorder (ADHD), dyslexia, physical, sensory and cognitive impairments, behavioural, emotional and social difficulties and other identified or non-identified learning difficulties (DfE 2013). Since the enactment of the Children and Families Act 2014, school-based and post-16 education professionals have shared the same terminology and definitions of special educational needs and learning difficulties as set out in the SEND COP (Introduction xiv).

The Department of Health (2001) information clarifies that it is a subset of young people receiving support through the SEND COP who may be considered to lack capacity to make a decision. Despite the unfamiliar wording of the Stage 1 question, the functional approach of the Department of Health learning disability definition is familiar. Education professionals working with a young person are aware of how they learn, their rate of learning, their progress acquiring new skills, as well as their ability to understand new or complex information. This will inform how work is planned and delivered for the young person, and form part of any recording of progress. Staff will also have knowledge of the young person's speech, language and communication skills, as well as being aware of how the young person functions socially in different settings within the educational establishment. Ascertaining if the young person's difficulties began before their 18th birthday can be resolved if they are, or were, the subject of an EHC Plan, or from reports or information provided by the schools or colleges attended, prior to 18+ provision. Talking with the young person's parent/carer may also assist. Thus, it is possible for education professionals to consider a young person in terms of the 'learning disability' definition.

## Mental health issues

Education professionals know about learning difficulties, but are understandably less likely to be well informed about mental health issues. The Children and Families Act 2014 introduced mental health difficulties as an area of SEN in association with social and emotional difficulties (SEND COP 6.32). This section provides a few examples of behaviours that may be indicative of an underlying mental health difficulty. More detailed information and guidance is offered in the DfE publication *Mental Health and Behaviour in Schools* (June 2014). Although this document is aimed at schools, the information in Annexes A and C about young people's mental health problems is taken from the accepted classification of mental health (e.g. ICD10) issues used by both adolescent and adult mental health professionals. These include:

- depression

- anxiety: generalised anxiety, panic disorder, habit disorders such as obsessive-compulsive disorder, phobias and post-traumatic stress disorder

- bipolar disorder

- psychotic disorders, for example, schizophrenia

- hyperkinetic disorders: disturbance of activity and attention, for example, ADHD

- mental and behavioural disorders caused by psychoactive substance misuse, for example, cannabis
- eating disorders
- autism
- personality and behavioural changes caused by brain injury
- deliberate self-harm.

The Chief Medical Officer's report (2012) (published 2013) notes that 75% of adult mental health illness have shown by the time a young person is 18 years old. It is now recognised that adolescence to early adulthood is the main time for the onset of mental health problems (Mental Health Foundation undated). According to the Royal College of Psychiatrists website,[1] one in four people will experience a mental health problem during a year. Mental health issues are considered one of the UK's biggest health problems alongside cancer. Thus, it is very likely that education professionals working with this age group will encounter young people with mental health problems. An indication of the prevalence of mental health issues in the 16–24 age group comes from Young Minds (2015)[2] citing figures gleaned from a number of sources, but mainly from a study published in 2009. It found that 2.2% of young people are likely to experience a depressive episode, 3.6% generalised anxiety, 2.3% obsessive-compulsive disorder, 0.2% psychotic disorders and 8.9% self-harm. Additionally, 36% of young people with learning disabilities also experience mental health problems. Approximately 21% of males and 18% of females drink more than the recommended alcohol units per week.

Whilst some young people with mental health problems will be receiving support and possibly a diagnosis, others will not. Despite the inclusion of mental health difficulties as an area of need in the

---

1  www.rcpsych.ac.uk/pdf/Position%20Statement%204%20website.pdf.
2  www.youngminds.org.uk/training_services/policy/useful_statistic/young_adults_statistics.

SEND COP, educationalists are, understandably, not trained in mental health. Although many will have experience of mental health problems through partners, relatives, friends or colleagues, this is unlikely to provide the range of knowledge assumed by the Stage 1 capacity assessment question. As noted in Chapter 2, the MCA and MCA COP were written with health and social care professionals in mind, all of who routinely have some level of training in mental health issues.

In the absence of guidance and preparation, knowing the difference between what is a mental health problem and what is just a young person's way of being, is likely to be challenging. The MindEd website,[3] set up by a number of medical Royal Colleges and the British Psychological Society, offers 'a free educational resource on children and young people's mental health for adults'. It covers the age range 0–18 years. It provides information about a range of common mental health problems, and gives a perspective on what is normal behaviour, and what is a concern.

Nevertheless, websites are not always maintained and, therefore, may not have longevity. The Royal College of Psychiatrists has always offered leaflets for young people and those caring for them, now downloadable, covering a range of mental health problems, but not the warning signs. Young Minds, a charity that focuses on improving emotional wellbeing and mental health, covers the age range 0–25 years, offering advice and information to young people, parents and professionals. Its HeadMeds website provides young people with information about the 21 most common mental health conditions and medications (see the Resources section at the end of this book).

The American Psychiatric Association (APA) website sets out a list of early warning signs of mental illness, advising that there needs to be several of these signs present to indicate a serious problem. It emphasises that these cannot predict a mental illness, but if a young person is presenting with a number of these signs, they should be

---

3   www.minded.org.uk/index.php.

encouraged to seek professional help. The APA acknowledges that education staff may be the first to notice changes in behaviour.

The early warning signs are:

- Recent social withdrawal and loss of interest in others.

- An unusual drop in functioning, especially at school or work, such as quitting sports, failing in school, or difficulty performing familiar tasks.

- Problems with concentration, memory, or logical thought and speech that are hard to explain.

- Heightened sensitivity to sights, sounds, smells or touch; avoidance of over-stimulating situations.

- Loss of initiative or desire to participate in any activity; apathy.

- A vague feeling of being disconnected from oneself or one's surroundings; a sense of unreality.

- Unusual or exaggerated beliefs about personal powers to understand meanings or influence events; illogical or 'magical' thinking typical of childhood in an adult.

- Fear or suspiciousness of others or a strong nervous feeling.

- Uncharacteristic, peculiar behaviour.

- Dramatic sleep and appetite changes or deterioration in personal hygiene.

- Rapid or dramatic shifts in feelings or 'mood swings'.

(APA 2014)

### Emotional wellbeing issues

There is an overlap between emotional wellbeing and mental health issues. The SEND COP (6.32) links together social, emotional and mental health difficulties, noting that the difficulties are exhibited in many ways, such as becoming withdrawn or socially isolated, or as challenging, disruptive or disturbing behaviour, such as defiance, aggression or anti-social behaviour. Education professionals are very familiar with behavioural problems, and having a perspective on whether this is usual adolescent/young adult behaviours or something different.

The APA checklist identifies social or emotional behaviours that may be a concern. The National Children's Bureau has published a best practice framework for schools to promote wellbeing and respond to mental health issues (see Weare 2015). Whilst aimed at schools, the information and advice is relevant to post-16 staff and establishments. It addresses the misuse of social media and cyberbullying, which are now recognised as a major contributor to emotional disorders.

## Acquired brain injury

Acquired brain injury refers to brain injury acquired after birth through accidents, known as traumatic brain injury, or infections or strokes or tumours. The MCA COP (4.12) examples of impairment or disturbance of the functioning of the brain or mind include the long-term effects of brain damage.

According to the charity Headway's website,[4] there are 10,000–20,000 severe traumatic brain injuries per year in the UK. The 15–24 age group is most at risk, and males are twice as likely as females to sustain a severe traumatic brain injury. Brain injury can affect aspects of cognitive, emotional, behavioural and physical functioning. Young people may develop mental health problems, which may be part of the head injury or a reaction to their changed state. This suggests that post-16 educational professionals may occasionally be working with a young person who has acquired difficulties resulting from a head injury, having previously had no SEN. Educational establishment staff should ensure that they are aware of how the young person's head injury affects their functioning, and that the effects depend on the area(s) of the brain that have been injured.

---

4   Available at www.headway.org.uk/About-traumatic-brain-injury.aspx.

## Summary of the findings

At the outset, the language and concepts of the two capacity assessment questions seemed alien, but through a convoluted route, some have been found to be very familiar. The concept of learning disabilities, using the Department of Health (2001) functional definition, falls well within the knowledge and expertise of education professionals. Equally, the Department of Health's helpful clarification that not all young people receiving support under the SEND COP will meet the MCA COP criteria for it to be considered they may lack capacity to make a particular decision facilitates education professionals focusing their attention on those young people who are more likely to lack capacity to make a particular decision (see Appendix 2). However, it may still be unclear which young people may meet the MCA COP criteria for it to be considered they lack capacity. In direct contravention of the MCA COP's stipulation that a judgement about lacking capacity should not be made based on SEN, labels and diagnoses, but to assist education professionals, the author suggests that young people who are likely to lack capacity are those receiving educational provision in establishments, or following courses, catering for young people with profound and multiple, severe or significant learning difficulties. However, young people attending any educational establishment may experience mental health problems that affect their decision-making ability. On the other hand, a young person who has achieved GCSEs or other recognised academic qualifications, regardless of their SEN, is very unlikely to lack capacity to make a decision. Young people who are on the autistic spectrum may pose particular challenges.

Statistics giving the prevalence of mental health problems indicate that this is a relatively common problem, but educationalists' lack of training in this area means it is likely to be a challenging issue. For reference, it takes eight years to train as a clinical or educational psychologist and 13 years to be a consultant psychiatrist.

Although there is DfE education-focused guidance in this area, it is for schools, and not post-16 establishments. The Department of Health funded MindEd website provides information up to the age of 18; the Royal College of Psychiatrists and the charity Young Minds offer information about mental health problems for young people aged 18+.

It is unfortunate that neither the SEND COP nor the MCA COP provides all the necessary information. Nevertheless, this can be located in a range of documents and information published by the DfE, Department of Health, Young Minds, the National Children's Bureau and other professional organisations' websites.

## Step-by-step guide to undertaking a capacity assessment

### Does the young person require a capacity assessment for this decision?

The first step is to establish whether the young person meets the Stage 1 question criteria. The flow chart below shows the process to do this.

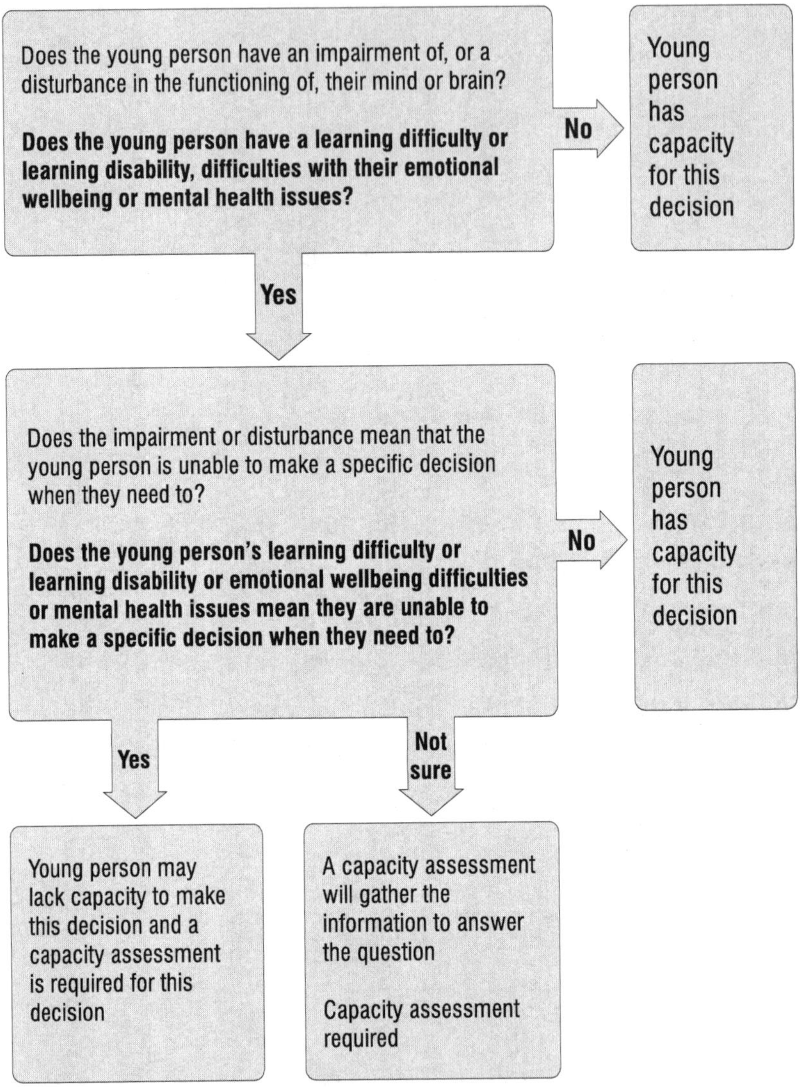

**Figure 4.1** Flow chart to determine if a young person requires a capacity assessment for a particular decision

If the outcome is that a capacity assessment is required for this decision, careful consideration will need to be given to the planning and conduct of the assessment.

The person carrying out the assessment is known as the *assessor*.

## Who should assess a young person's capacity to make a particular decision?

The MCA COP (4.38) states that it is usually the person who needs the young person to make the decision who assesses their capacity to do this. It notes that this will be different people for different decisions. Thus, in relation to educational matters, depending on the decision, this could be a member of school or college staff, a specialist teacher, or a local authority officer. For example, for a decision about support or specialist equipment, it may be a tutor/teacher or specialist tutor/teacher. For decisions concerning the content of an EHC Plan, including a change of educational placement or a personal budget request, it could be the relevant local authority officer. It will be different education professionals depending on the type of decision to be made.

Generally, decisions about proposed amendments to an EHC Plan are made during the annual review process, which focuses on the outcomes, support and any amendments (SEND COP 9.176). A local authority representative might attend the annual review meeting. Regardless of their attendance, it is the local authority's decision whether to accept these proposals and amend the EHC Plan, as it has overall responsibility for maintaining it. Until the end of Year 11 (Y11), it is the young person's parents, with the educational establishment staff, who suggest amendments, but from then young people have the right to make decisions about the content of their EHC Plan. For some young people, there may be concerns about their ability to make such decisions, and this may need to be formally considered through a capacity assessment.

The requirement set out in the SEND COP (9.175) that the educational institution leads the annual review is, in effect, delegating the local authority's responsibility to ascertain the young person's capacity to make decisions about the content of an EHC Plan, to the educational institution staff. As noted in Chapter 2, the MCA COP presumes training or experience working with the people who may lack capacity. This is not necessarily the case for local authority officers, who may have minimal or no experience of directly working with young people with SEN. Thus, it would seem appropriate that educational establishment staff, who know the young person, are the most appropriate professionals to establish the young person's ability to make suggestions about the content of their EHC Plan. However, any proposals would be subject to the local authority's agreement. Nevertheless, consideration has to be given as to whether this arrangement complies with the MCA COP (4.38), which establishes who 'usually' assesses a young person's ability to make the specific decision. The inclusion of 'usually' suggests it is probably acceptable for the local authority to delegate the determination of a young person's decision-making capacity, in relation to their EHC Plan, to the educational establishment staff.

This discussion may be regarded as pedantry. Nonetheless, laws have to be operated fairly and justly for and by those to whom it applies. Thus, it is important to establish that the requirements in one law are compatible with the specifications in another that is to be operated with it; otherwise, this could leave education professionals and young people in a legal limbo. Whilst the Children and Families Act 2014 was written to include the MCA, it was evident from the flawed Annex 1 in the SEND COP published in July 2014, and not amended for re-publication in January 2015, that those drafting it were not conversant with the MCA. Therefore, exploring the compatibility of requirements between the two laws is necessary to ensure educational professionals, and young people, are not placed in difficult situations.

### Local authority officers as assessors

As noted above, unlike educational establishment staff or specialist teachers and educational psychologists, local authority officers may have minimal or no experience or training in working with young people with SEN. Therefore, it is appropriate to consider how a local authority officer may be enabled to comply with the MCA requirements, without putting the young person at a disadvantage. There may be circumstances when delegating the responsibility of ascertaining the young person's understanding of a matter is not appropriate, as the local authority officer who requires the decision to be made, for example, considering whether to allocate a personal budget, needs to discuss this directly with the young person. In this situation, it would be recommended that the local authority officer work with someone from the educational establishment who knows the young person. This may be more challenging if the young person attends an out-of-district educational establishment, but could be overcome by communicating with the young person via Skype or other VOIP software. The young person would have to be carefully prepared for this form of communication. The advantage of Skype/VOIP is that it allows the use of visual means of communication as well as verbal.

Collaborating with someone from the educational establishment who knows the young person would ensure the young person:

- is prepared for the meeting
- is presented with information in their preferred format
- understands the language being used
- can be understood by the local authority officer
- is given time to process the information
- communicates with the local authority officer in a familiar place
- can have someone with them to support them if they wish, in addition to the member of staff.

Given the emphasis on the co-production of EHC Plans, local authority officers would be advised to meet and get to know the young people whose EHC Plans they manage. This would assist young people in understanding the abstract concept of the local authority, as it would have a human representation. The issues related to this are discussed later in this chapter, in the 'Using the "four key questions"' section.

## Other professionals: psychologists, psychiatrists, speech and language therapists

The 'usually' in the MCA COP (4.38) raises the issue of the role of other professionals in assessing a young person's capacity for educational matters. As noted in Chapter 2, the MCA and MCA COP were written with health and social care professionals in mind. In health, it is clear that the treating professional requires the young person to make the decision; therefore, the healthcare professional is the person who assesses the young person's capacity to consent to the treatment. If the healthcare professional requires advice from a clinical psychologist or psychiatrist, the status of this assistance is a specialist opinion, enabling the treating healthcare professional to make a judgement about a young person's capacity to consent to treatment. Consequently, this suggests that sometimes an education professional may need advice from another professional, such as a speech and language therapist or educational psychologist (EP), to assist them in determining a young person's capacity to make a particular decision. Ultimately, it will be the assessor's decision, taking account of any professional advice or information, as to whether the young person has capacity.

As noted above, local authority officers can be considered a special case, and may need more active assistance from an education professional who knows the young person, to ensure the MCA Principle 2 (all the help and support) is upheld. In addition, advice may also need to be sought from another professional.

## *Are there considerations to be aware of when undertaking the role of assessor?*

Some education professionals may be concerned about the ethics of undertaking a capacity assessment, as the outcome may deprive a young person of their right to make their own decision. For educationalists, the harsh approach of the MCA, in having no half measures, may sit very uncomfortably in a system used to being encouraging and accepting of 'nearly there'. This is a reasonable position, as, when introducing the MCA into the SEND COP, it has added another layer of complexity for a young person to understand in relation to decisions about the content of an EHC Plan – the abstract concept of the local authority.

In health and social care, people are offered definite choices that are not usually dependent on the agreement of a third party. Thus, a doctor discussing treatment options is talking about certainties, the patient choosing something that will definitely happen. When a young person suggests amendments to their EHC Plan or requests an educational placement, these happening are dependent on the local authority agreeing them, which may be challenging for a young person with special needs to comprehend. Theoretically, to be considered to have capacity to make the decision, the young person will have to show that they know that their choice is dependent on the agreement of the local authority. Potentially, this could mean a young person who is able to make a decision about an outcome or provision, or choice of educational placement, they wish to have written into the EHC Plan, being deemed to lack capacity because they do not understand the need for the local authority's agreement. This would seem to be unfair and not in keeping with the spirit of the MCA. Is there a pragmatic and legally acceptable solution to this dilemma? The author puts forward a proposal in the 'Using the "four key questions"' section below.

As noted earlier in the book, there may be some 'more serious and significant decisions' that do not form part of an EHC Plan, and therefore do not entail the agreement of a third party, for example, choosing options within courses or work experience placements. In these instances, the young person is being offered something that if they choose it, this is what they will be doing.

So, are there concerns about considering if the young person has the capacity to make the decision? Some may feel there is a tension between the role of educator and assessor of a young person's capacity. The role of assessor is not unusual for educators, and a young person not being awarded their expected grade can have far-reaching consequences. Those working with young people with SEN have to evaluate and record progress, so are accustomed to making judgements about ability. Perhaps it is the emphasis on the legality of the process that is causing concern, or potentially being in conflict with the young person, or more probably, their parents, if there is disagreement about the outcome. Reframing it casts the education professional as the young person's champion, proving that they can make their own decisions, despite their parents' anxieties.

The first quote in Chapter 1 epitomises parents' concerns about their young person with SEN making their own decisions. The MCA COP supports education professionals endeavouring to facilitate a young person making their own decision. The MCA COP Chapter 6 explains how an education professional is protected in carrying out their responsibilities under the MCA, if they have followed the guidance. The MCA COP Chapter 4 explains how to undertake a capacity assessment, emphasising the importance of doing this correctly (4.34). It advises about ensuring the principles of the MCA have been applied (4.64), and the good practice of keeping formal records (4.61). Therefore, following the processes laid out in the MCA COP provides the protection and evidence for the decision about a young person's capacity to make the particular choice.

Essentially, education professionals do not really have a choice about whether to become involved with a young person's capacity to make a particular educational decision, as they have to have regard to the SEND and MCA COPs. Nonetheless, they do have control about how it is done; this is the most important aspect, in terms of ensuring a young person is enabled to make their own decisions wherever possible.

### Local authority officers

The MCA COP (4.43) states that 'any assessor should have the skills and ability to communicate effectively with the person. If necessary, they should get professional help to communicate with the person' (p.54). Local authority officers need to be aware of and reflect on their level of training and experience in working with young people with SEN, and consider if it would enable them to discuss the choices with the young person in a way they would be able to understand. Making a judgement about a young person's capacity to make the particular decision is, in effect, a legal process, the outcome of which can be challenged by the young person, their parents or another professional.

## *Attributes required by the assessor*
### Training

Those who have to have regard to the MCA COP range from highly qualified professionals to care workers. Thus, whilst formal qualifications are not required, experience of working directly with those who may lack capacity, training in the MCA principles and capacity assessments are essential.

Within education, there is a range of people who may need to be able to undertake an assessment of a young person's ability to make a particular decision. This is likely to include teachers, college tutors, school or college support staff, such as teaching or learning assistants, communication support workers, interveners, local authority officers and EPs. Regardless of their training and experience, or lack of it, in working with young people with SEN, *all* will need training about the MCA principles and undertaking capacity assessments.

When the MCA was enacted, the Department of Health published training materials and guidance. Since then many professional training courses include the MCA and capacity assessments. Additionally, some professional organisations such as the British Medical Association provide online resources. Other roles receive their training in a variety of ways. Many local authorities have online resources and training materials, as well as the Social Care Institute for Excellence's (SCIE) free e-learning modules, designed for people working in health and social care. Similar resources for those working in education have yet to be developed.

## Know the young person: factors to consider

It is highly desirable that the assessor and young person know each other. This is in accord with the essence of the MCA Principle 2, having all the help and support possible to make and communicate a decision. A capacity assessment is based in law; the outcome either allows or denies a young person their right. Therefore, it is essential that a capacity assessment is conducted in a manner that does not disadvantage the young person. The assessor's knowledge of the young person is fundamental to facilitating a fair assessment of the young person's decision-making capacity. Since the MCA takes a functional approach, 'know' encompasses an awareness of the way the young person functions. Within an educational establishment it should be easily arranged that the assessor and young person are known to each other. Ideally, this should form part of any guidelines drawn up by the establishment for carrying out capacity assessments.

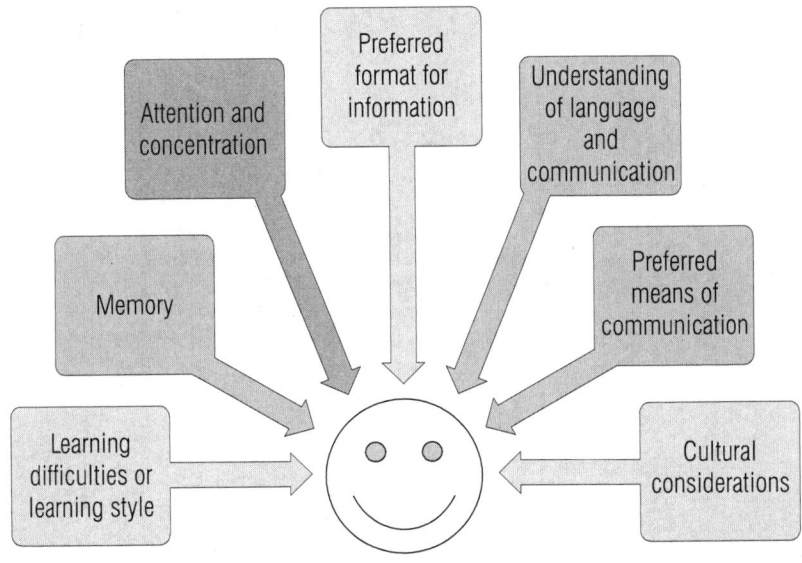

**Figure 4.2** Factors to be considered by the assessor when undertaking a capacity assessment

The functional assessment of capacity is based on the young person's ability to understand and remember the information, use it to help make the decision and then communicate their response. However, the young person's language and communication abilities, along with learning difficulties and learning style, are overarching factors. Other issues such as attention and concentration, or cultural matters, may also affect the way a young person functions.

## Language and Communication

The MCA COP (3.4) states that 'good communication is essential for explaining relevant information in an appropriate way and for ensuring that the steps being taken meet an individual's need' (p.30).

A capacity assessment is an interaction between the assessor and the young person. It is not a test or exam, nor is it something done to the young person; it is an enabling process. Like all exchanges, it is mediated by language, verbally and/or non-verbally. The assessor's knowledge of the young person's understanding of language and communication is key to planning and conducting a fair assessment, as well as their ability to use a range of communication strategies. For example, a young person may have a limited vocabulary, or a literal understanding of language, or require signing or augmented communication. The young person may have adopted particular words or phrases, signs or pictures to refer to the choices. The MCA COP (3.10) offers some general basic guidance about communication, which will be routine to education professionals, such as using simple language accompanied with visual supports, breaking down information into smaller chunks and repeating information as well as pausing to check understanding. It also highlights speaking at the right volume and speed.

Part of a capacity assessment involves the young person being able to communicate their choice by any means. Equally important is the assessor's ability to understand the young person's communication style, as this could make the --difference between being considered to have, or lack, capacity for this decision. If the young person has understood the information, retained and used it to make a choice, but their way of indicating their preference is not recognised by the assessor, leading to the conclusion that the young person lacks capacity, this would be unfair. This is illustrated by the following two scenarios.

> Jill is an 18-year-old further education (FE) college student with Down's syndrome. She communicates using Makaton signing and saying some single words, mostly unintelligible to those unfamiliar with her speech.

She enjoys using her iPad to take photos, play games and to assist her communication. Jill likes looking after animals. She has a cat, which she feeds daily, and helps her parents clean out the family's hamster.

Jill is following a life skills course and has to choose between an animal care or horticulture option with related work experience. As Jill's tutor (Mrs Jones) has a concern about Jill's ability to make this decision, she decides a capacity assessment is required. Jill has been using the signs for flower and cat, accompanying her signing with an unintelligible 'flower' and clearly spoken 'cat'.

Scenario 1: The departmental policy is that the head of department (Mrs Stocks) always undertakes capacity assessments regardless of whether the student knows her, or that she is able to communicate with the student. Mrs Stocks does not know Makaton. Jill has seen Mrs Stocks but does not know her. She meets with Jill, verbally explains, and shows her all the information, including the video of her visiting the two work experience placements. Mrs Stocks believed Jill demonstrated that she understood the information as she was able to use her iPad to show what she thought was good about each of the choices. Mrs Stocks asked Jill to say which option she was choosing, Jill said and signed something, but Mrs Stocks was not able to understand. Mrs Stocks concluded that as Jill was unable to communicate her choice, on the balance of probabilities, she lacked capacity to make this decision.

Scenario 2: The departmental policy is that the member of staff who knows the student well, especially their communication needs, undertakes the capacity assessment for decisions about matters related to the course or college. Mrs Jones is a proficient Makaton signer and is very familiar with Jill's way of communicating. Mrs Jones meets with Jill and explains the choice through simple language supported with Makaton signs as well as showing her all the information including the video of her visiting the two work experience placements. Mrs

Jones believed Jill demonstrated that she understood the information as she was able to use her iPad to show what she thought was good about each of the choices. Mrs Jones asked Jill to indicate which option she was choosing, Jill said and signed 'flower'. Although surprised by the choice, Mrs Jones understood that Jill had picked the horticulture option. Mrs Jones was satisfied that Jill had demonstrated that, on the balance of probabilities, she had the capacity to make this decision.

### Format for information

Presenting the information in the most appropriate format for the young person is central to a fair assessment of a young person's capacity to make a particular decision. Being aware of the young person's learning style, and preferences for receiving information, enables the assessor to facilitate the young person's decision-making. For example, a young person may like to see photos or other visual media, or use objects of reference, to help understand spoken or signed language. Some young people's understanding is enhanced by actually experiencing the matters under consideration. If the decision relates to a change of educational placement, it would be expected that the young person has visited the establishments under consideration. Again, giving information in an inappropriate form or not visiting the choice of educational placements would be unfair to the young person, as it could lead to a determination that they lack capacity.

Examples in this book suggest using tablet computers and other electronic devices to gather and present information in a range of media. Many young people with SEN engage well with this technology. However, when using tablet computers etc. for this purpose, the information must be regularly backed up, for example, on another computer or memory stick, in case anything happens to the particular device, so all is not lost.

### Memory, concentration and attention

Whilst memory forms a component of the capacity assessment, to reiterate, the capacity assessment is not an exam; the young person can have the information shown to them or repeated as many times as required. This is embedded in the second principle of the MCA – a young person should be given all the help and support possible to make a decision. Nevertheless, any difficulties the young person experiences with attention and concentration may have an impact on their performance. However, the assessor's knowledge of the young person will be foremost in ensuring the capacity assessment is planned and undertaken, taking account of any weakness in attention and concentration. For example, if the young person's attention and concentration wanes towards lunchtime or mid-afternoon, then a capacity assessment should be undertaken at a time of day when the young person is likely to be most alert. Medical conditions such as diabetes or epilepsy can affect concentration and attention, which may have an impact on the young person's functioning. The assessor may need to plan the timing of a capacity assessment flexibly to take account of the young person's level of alertness.

### Cultural considerations

This is culture in its broadest sense, encompassing social, religious and cultural factors. Everyone experiences these in some measure, but the influence they exert over a person's decision-making will vary between individuals, but can also be changeable within the same person depending on circumstances. For example, a Jewish young person may regularly buy a bacon sandwich when there is no one from the community present, but choose tuna fish when someone from the community is in the same café.

Clothing and accessories can be part of culture – this ranges from dress for religious reasons to having clothing or a hairstyle denoting the membership of or following a particular social or cultural grouping. Knowing the young person means the assessor may be aware of how important particular issues are to the young person, and have regard to these when planning and undertaking a capacity assessment, or considering the outcome. The MCA is about making one's own decision. Whilst a young person's choice may have taken into account a range of considerations, it is important that the assessor believes that the young person's choice is their own, and not one they have been forced to make.

This book is concerned with educational decisions. However, educational establishment staff may become aware that decisions are being made by others, on the young person's behalf in their family life. Educational professions would be advised to familiarise themselves with the decisions, set out in the MCA and MCA COP (1.10), that others cannot make on behalf of a young person who lacks capacity, including consenting to marriage or civil partnership, consenting to sexual relations, or consenting to a child being placed for adoption. Additionally, since June 2014, forced marriage has become a criminal offence in England and Wales. In the case of a young person who lacks capacity to consent to marriage, the criteria of coercion in relation to forced marriage does not apply.

OTHER FACTORS THAT MAY AFFECT A YOUNG PERSON'S PERFORMANCE

The MCA COP (4.46) emphasises that young people should be in the 'best state' to make the particular decision required; consequently, the assessor will need to be aware of any factors that may be affecting the young person's functioning.

As noted above, certain medical conditions may affect a young person's capabilities. Some over-the-counter or prescription medications can affect performance, for example, medication for hay fever or other allergies that cause drowsiness. Ideally, the assessor would need to be aware of any medical issues that may impair a young person's functioning. However, this has to be balanced with the young person's right to privacy about health matters that are not part of their SEN.

The young person's emotional state may be easier to discern, although the reasons for any upset may be unknown. The assessor's knowledge of the young person will enable them to gauge the young person's mood. Occasionally, it may be appropriate to check how the young person is feeling at the time of the assessment, although expressing an emotional state can be very challenging for some young people, so visual prompts such as smiley and sad faces may assist.

## Other barriers to decision-making

A fundamental barrier to decision-making may be that the young person is uncertain about how to choose between the options. The SEND COP has a core principle about children and young people participating in making decisions from an early age. So it is hoped that by the time a young person is 16 years old they will have experience of making choices. To ensure this, it is suggested in Chapter 3 (this book), that decision-making could be considered as an outcome in an EHC Plan, or as part of a person-centred plan. It is also noted that this is advocated in the MCA COP (3.5).

A young person may be concerned about making the wrong choice. This may be related to their preference differing from their parents' preference. The MCA places an emphasis on the decision being the young person's own choice, and not one made under the influence of others.

Another factor may be related to the young person disliking change. Some educational decisions involve significant changes, such as moving educational placement, starting a different course, being supported in a different way, or being encouraged to travel independently. However, it is likely that the young person's attitude to change will be well known to educational establishment staff and the appropriate support given.

Occasionally the young person may not like any of the choices on offer, but perhaps does not know what it is they would prefer. This is probably a rare event.

## Know the relevant information for the decision

First and foremost, the assessor needs to be very clear about what decision it is that the young person is required to make. The assessor must know the information about the choices, including advantages and disadvantages, because a key part of a capacity assessment entails the assessor discussing and explaining the information to the young person. Being unable to present all the facts will disadvantage the young person in their efforts to make the choice. The MCA COP (4.16) states that quick or inadequate explanations are not acceptable, but notes in 3.9 that giving too much detail may be confusing. The key is not to omit important information. A young person needs to understand the essential information or concepts. Determining what is important is decision-dependent – for example, when choosing a new educational placement the young person must be able to identify, verbally or non-verbally, the different establishments under consideration.

As most 'more serious and significant' educational decisions are known in advance, the assessor needs to ensure that they are aware of all the information relating to the particular decision. The local authority Local Offer (see the Glossary) should be consulted, as this documents what is provided by the local authority and others, for example, in terms of post-16 education and training provision, apprenticeships, traineeships and supported internships, and travel arrangements to and from post-16 institutions (SEND COP 4.30).

If the young person is choosing to attend a new placement outside the local authority area, there may be details about this in the Local Offer, as local authorities have to record out-of-district provision that is likely to be used by young people, such as FE colleges in neighbouring areas. Furthermore, the Local Offer should provide information about regional and national specialist provision available, such as for low incidence or complex SEN (SEND COP 4.4).

Additionally, the local authority may have produced information specifically for young people with SEN about some decisions, such as personal budgets or moving educational placement.

As noted above, some educational decisions have an additional factor – understanding that the local authority's agreement is required. This is discussed below in the 'Using the "four key questions"' section.

## *Considerations when planning a capacity assessment*

Attributes of the assessor have been explored in depth, but equally important is the way in which the assessment is conducted, as this could affect the reliability and validity of the outcome. It is essential that factors affecting functioning, or that place the young person at a disadvantage, are considered. The Mental Health Foundation (undated) and the British Psychological Society and SCIE (2010) have developed audit tools to help an assessor reflect on their assessment; the former is designed for anyone undertaking a capacity assessment, the latter for professionals. The items encourage the assessor to think about communication, the presentation of information, as well as the environment, putting the person at ease, and cultural and religious considerations. Hence, planning a capacity assessment should include where (environment) and when (timing) the assessment will be undertaken, and the manner (how) in which it will be conducted, including technology or equipment for use by the assessor and/or young person. The assessor may find it helpful to devise a checklist to assist them in planning and carrying out a capacity assessment (see Appendix 1 for a sample capacity assessment planning checklist).

### Where (environment)?

A capacity assessment is confidential and the young person has a right to privacy. The capacity assessment should take place somewhere that:

- offers the young person privacy

- the young person feels at ease in – generally this will be somewhere familiar to the young person

- has appropriate seating and a table; if the young person has a sensory impairment, it may necessitate the assessor sitting in a particular position relative to the young person, for example, opposite, and so the seating arrangement must allow for this

- meets the needs of young people with sensory impairments. It is important to ensure that the lighting or noise levels are suitable. Guidance about these may be set out in the EHC Plan or have been given by specialist staff

- is wheelchair accessible and enables the wheelchair to be positioned appropriately

- is big enough to comfortably accommodate all those who need to be present

- enables the good practice for assessments of letting the young person sit nearest the door so they do not feel trapped

- is not too hot or cold and well ventilated, with the means to block any glare from the sun

- has plug sockets, internet and intranet access and mobile network connection, if these are likely to be required.

## When (timing)?

- Many of the 'more serious or significant' educational decisions a young person will be required to make will be known well ahead of the date they are actually needed. Annual review meetings are scheduled several weeks if not months in advance, giving ample time to plan capacity assessment for decisions related to this. As noted above, the young person needs to be in the right frame of mind, and so it is advisable to schedule a capacity assessment in good time to accommodate any variability in the young person's functioning. For example, some young people have poor sleep patterns, which may affect their functioning.

- If the young person is required to make more than one decision for which their capacity to make the particular decision is uncertain, it would be advisable to set aside separate sessions for each decision.

- The assessor needs to ensure that they allocate sufficient time for the assessment. Most capacity assessments for 'more serious or significant' decisions cannot be undertaken quickly. Enough time must be allowed for explaining and showing the young person the information – working with language interpreters, including sign language, or an intervener, will lengthen the time needed. Some young people process information slowly and/or take time to respond, and this needs to be considered when allotting time.

- A capacity assessment should be arranged at the time of day when the young person is most alert. As noted above, a young person's attention and concentration may wane at certain times of the day. Some may tire as the week progresses, so a capacity assessment may need to be scheduled earlier rather than later in the week.

## How (manner)?

The generalities of how, rather than the specifics of using the 'four key questions', are discussed below.

### Working collaboratively: local authority officers and educational establishment staff

As noted above, some educational decisions require the young person to be aware that the local authority has to agree with their choices. Those related to placement and personal budgets necessitate the young person having an awareness of the local authority's role. It is advised that the relevant local authority officer works with staff from the young person's educational establishment to ensure that the second principle of the MCA (all the help and support possible) is upheld. The scenario below is presented as food for thought; consider the way in which the MCA principles are upheld, particularly Principle 2.

---

Ms Joseph, the local authority SEN officer, manages Jill's EHC Plan. Prior to taking up her current post ten years ago, she was a special educational needs coordinator (SENCo) in a mainstream primary school. Whilst Ms Joseph has teenage children of her own, she has minimal experience of working directly with young people with significant learning disabilities. She met Jill three years ago, but not since, and is aware she will need assistance from the staff at Jill's school to ascertain if Jill is able to choose which college she attends. Ms Joseph contacts the school at the start of the new school year, as college choices have to be submitted to the local authority by mid-January, to plan how Jill will make the choice. The school inform Ms Joseph they will be:

- setting up a meeting with Jill to look at all the choices for college, including residential special colleges, as well as plan how to help Jill gather the information she needs

- obtaining Jill's consent to invite her parents to this meeting so they can support the process

- introducing Jill and, with her consent, her parents to the local authority materials about choosing a new placement and the role of the local authority. These resources cover the local authority policy of encouraging independent travel as well as how it makes decisions about requests for residential special colleges

- preparing Jill for and arranging visits to the colleges. Preparation will help Jill to know what it is she wants to find out about the college, such as where the students eat lunch, what is on offer for lunch, the location of the toilets, if there are activities such as riding for the disabled, as well as what she will learn. These are prompts in the local authority booklet about choosing a new educational placement. Jill will be encouraged to take photos of the answers to her questions, as well as audio recording of answers.

Ms Joseph thinks school staff are the best people to decide whether Jill is able to make her own decision. However, she is aware that the abstract notion of the local authority having to agree the choice may adversely affect Jill's ability to make the choice. To assist school staff, Ms Joseph suggests they use her photo to represent the local authority and she will have a Skype chat with Jill nearer the time she has to make her decision. Jill is used to talking to someone over Skype — her older brother is away at university and he communicates with Jill in this way during term time. Ms Joseph hopes that this will facilitate Jill's understanding about the local authority and its preferences. She will also explain, in simple terms, that the local authority like young people to attend the nearest college that offers a suitable course, as there is a policy of encouraging young people to travel independently. If Jill is considering residential specialist college, Ms Joseph will talk about how the local authority thinks about such a request. She suggests that, with Jill's consent, Jill's parents are present at this 'meeting'.

When Jill has made her decision, Ms Joseph suggests another meeting possibly via Skype or in person, depending on time, so Jill can tell Ms Joseph her choice and the reasons for it. Ms Joseph believes this meeting should take place, regardless of whether Jill has been considered to have the capacity to make the decision, so she is aware of Jill's wishes and feelings. If Jill has been deemed not to have the capacity to make the choice, then her parents will be doing this on her behalf and must act in Jill's 'best interests', which includes taking account of Jill's wishes and feelings.

Local authority officers may wish to consider producing easy-to-understand materials about choosing educational placements and personal budgets for young people that could be used by educational establishment staff and parents to prepare young people to make their decision. This could include podcasts, videos, booklets and online materials.

### Discussions with parents, educational establishment staff and other professionals

The MCA COP (4.49) suggests that the assessor may need other relevant information to support their assessment. This may be background information from parents, but not their views, wishes or the choice they would make. The quotes from parents at the beginning of Chapter 1 suggest they will probably find it challenging not to state their wishes, feelings or choice, but it is important that the outcome of the assessor's assessment is not influenced by parental views.

Educational establishment staff, or other professionals, may hold useful information about what decisions the young person has been making, and any observations about behavioural responses to matters related to the choice under consideration.

### Equipment

The assessor will need:

- capacity assessment record form and guidance notes, online or paper version

- capacity assessment ground rules poster (see Appendix 1), and Blu-Tack to put it on the wall so it can be easily seen by all in the room

- the young person's favoured representation of the local authority

- pen and paper or other means of note-taking, including audio and/or video recording.

The assessor may require:

- laptop, or tablet computer, as the young person's photos, videos, etc. relating to the decision may be stored on it. Possibly the supporting visual material may be cached on the educational establishment's server, so access to this will also be needed

- mobile phone, if this assists the young person's communication by responding through text messages

- specialist equipment, or access to specialised software, for young people with sensory impairments or physical disabilities

- smiley/sad face, or other visual representations of feelings, to check or monitor the young person's mood

- thumbs up, smiley face or other visual supports, and/ or rewards to provide encouragement to the young person during the capacity assessment

- help or advice from another professional, for example, speech and language therapist, educational psychologist

- an interpreter to assist the young person's communication, for example, sign language, intervener or first language.

The young person may require:

- laptop or tablet computer or augmented communication device

- mobile phone – if they will be using this to communicate their responses by text messaging

- glasses

- hearing aids – the assessor may need to check these are working and replace batteries as necessary.

### Putting the young person at ease

In addition to the above, the young person should be allowed to have someone with them to support them if they wish. This may be a friend, parent, other family member or member of staff. It is important to let the young person choose. Of equal importance is preparing the supporter for their role.

The MCA COP (2.8) raises the issue that someone supporting the young person may try to influence their decision. A factor could be the beliefs the supporter holds about the young person's capacity to make this decision. Possibly, the supporter may feel that the young person is unable to make choices due to the reasons they are considered to have SEN. Alternatively, like the parent in the first quote in Chapter 1, they may believe that, as they have a close relationship with their young person, they know what their young person wants. This could be a difficult situation to manage.

Some young people are bilingual and their supporter may prefer to communicate in their first language. This may present challenges to the assessor being sure the young person is making their own decision.

It is recommended that the assessor prepares the supporter for their role. The assessor will need to have some knowledge about the supporter, and their favoured way of accessing information. If the supporter is literate in English, perhaps one of the publications for parents about the MCA may be helpful in explaining that the young person should be enabled to make their own decision, even if it differs from the supporter's preference (see the References and Resources sections). The assessor may need to meet with the supporter in advance to explain the MCA and capacity assessment, as well as setting ground rules for the capacity assessment. Some supporters may try to give answers on behalf of the young person without giving them the opportunity to respond. Suggested ground rules are (see Appendix 1):

- Be patient, this process takes time.
- Switch off mobile phones unless they are needed to assist the young person's communication.
- The assessment is confidential.
- Reassure the young person there are no wrong answers.
- Let the young person communicate for him or herself, even if it takes them time to give a response.
- Give encouragement to the young person to respond.

## Using the 'four key questions'

If a capacity assessment is being undertaken, it *must* have been established that the young person meets the Stage 1 criteria to possibly lack capacity to make the particular decision about their education. That is, that they have a significant learning difficulty or disability, or emotional wellbeing or mental health problems. It is advisable to record full information about these on the capacity assessment form to show how the young person meets the Stage 1 criteria (see Appendix 1).

Prior to a capacity assessment being undertaken, it is expected that the young person will have been well prepared to make the particular decision. As most 'more serious and significant' educational decisions are known well in advance, it provides the opportunity to ensure the young person is aware they need to make a decision. It enables the young person to have been assisted to gather all the relevant information, in their preferred format, in readiness to make their choice.

The capacity assessment should not be the first time the young person is being presented with any of the information. The scenario below gives an example of how a young person may be prepared for making a decision about their educational placement.

> Jill attends her local special school, but she has to decide if she wants to remain in her current school for another year, or transfer to the local FE college for a life skills course. She has been attending the FE college for a day a week for the past year with other students and staff from her current school. In preparation for making the decision, the school staff have been talking with Jill, as well as assisting her use her iPad to take photos of key places and staff in each setting. School staff have used Jill's iPad to make some videos of her doing various activities in school and college. In addition, Jill has recorded her college tutor and school class teacher explaining and showing her what is on offer to her if she were to attend that educational establishment. This enables Jill to access the information when she wants to look at it. She is encouraged to show it to her parents so they can also talk to her about the choice she has to make. School staff have backed up all the information on Jill's iPad related to choosing her

educational placement on a weekly basis on school computer system under Jill's log-in and a memory stick that is kept securely in a locked filing cabinet.

It is good professional practice to formally record a capacity assessment using a capacity assessment record form, such as the one shown in Appendix 1, or the JAWS compatible version.[5] This is because the young person, their parent or other professional may question the outcome of a capacity assessment. If this occurs, the assessor must be able to demonstrate that they have applied the MCA principles (MCA COP 4.64) and can justify their conclusions (MCA COP 4.34). This issue is discussed in detail in Chapter 7.

The assessment and outcome relate to a specific decision at a particular time, and are confidential. Only the young person and those directly involved with the decision receive copies of the capacity assessment record form, and a copy should also be placed in the young person's file. The form is not to be circulated as part of general information about the young person, for example, as part of the annual review papers. If the outcome of the assessment concluded that the young person lacks capacity to make the particular decision, then the person who will decide on their behalf should also be given a copy. For educational decisions, this will generally be the young person's parent. When a capacity assessment has concluded that the young person has capacity to make the particular decision, the young person's consent is required to pass information from the assessment to their parents.

## Capacity assessment

At the start of the capacity assessment session the assessor should explain the ground rules, supported by a visual representation of these put up on a wall, or other surface, that can be easily seen by all.

When asking the young person questions, the MCA COP (4.49) indicates that those that can be answered with 'yes' or 'no' (closed questions) are to be avoided, although there is an acceptance that, for

---

5   See www.natsip.org.uk.

young people with significant communication difficulties, this may be the only way to elicit information. In this case, it is recommended to check the reliability of responses by asking the same question in a different way. For example, 'Do you like college X?' 'Do you want to go to college X?' 'Is college X the best college?'

Good practice, if there are concerns about the reliability of the capacity assessment, is to repeat the assessment a week or so later to see if the young person gives the same responses. If they do, this confirms the reliability of the assessment. If they give different answers, it raises questions about the validity of the outcome. Repeating it for a third time, a week or so later, may clarify the situation. If the young person gives different responses a third time, it is questionable that the young person has the capacity to make the decision.

> **Recap**
> - Capacity is either *Yes* or *No*; there is no such thing as partial capacity.
> - MCA 4.48 states that when there is doubt, the assessor must be able to show that it is more likely than not that the answer to the 'four key questions' is *No*.
> - The outcome of a capacity assessment is expressed as 'on the balance of probabilities, X has/lacks capacity to make this decision at this time'.

1. **Can the young person understand information *relevant* to the decision to be made?**

For the answer to be affirmative, the young person needs to understand the key facts/concepts, not all the fine details. The term 'relevant information' can be considered as referring to both general information about decision-making, and that which is specific to the particular decision. For every decision, the young person has to demonstrate they have a basic understanding about making this particular decision. The MCA COP (4.16) considers this as having an awareness of the following:

- *The nature of the decision.* What is the decision that has to be made, for example, to choose an educational establishment, a course, options within a course, outcomes and provision to be written into the EHC Plan, how support should be delivered, or taking part in an activity? The young person must be able to communicate to the assessor in some way that they know there is a choice to be made, and the options they have.

- *The reason why the decision is needed.* The young person should demonstrate a general understanding of the reason(s) the decision needs to be made. For example, if the young person is in their final year at their current establishment, they will need to show they understand that they are unable to continue attending. If they are selecting options, or work experience placements, the young person should show that they know that this is part of their course, and that they need to choose.

- *The likely effects of deciding one way or another, or making no decision at all.* The young person should be able to show a basic understanding that choosing one thing over another means they will not be doing or going to the other choices. For example, in the scenario above, Jill was choosing between her current school and attending college full time. If Jill's choice is college, she will need to demonstrate that she is aware that she will not be attending school, but going to college every day. Supposing Jill was picking options (for example, between horticulture and animal care) within a course, she would need to show she knows that choosing horticulture means she will not be doing any work with animals. In the event of Jill being unwilling, rather than unable, to make a decision, she will need to indicate she is aware there is a decision to be made and that, if she will not choose, someone else will do so for her.

There is no guidance in the MCA COP for the eventuality that a young person, whilst capable of making a decision, will not do so. However, it is envisaged this is likely to be an extremely rare occurrence. Nevertheless, should it happen, it is advisable to consider the possible barriers to decision-making discussed earlier in this chapter.

As noted above, for decisions related to the content of the young person's EHC Plan, it would appear that a young person has to demonstrate an awareness of the abstract concept of the local authority, and its role in managing the EHC Plan. This differs from decisions in health and social care, where the options offered are usually definite and not dependent on the approval of a third party. Seemingly, this adds another part to 'understanding the relevant information' that is likely to be very challenging for some young people. It may lead to a determination the young person lacks capacity, due to not understanding that the local authority has to agree the chosen amendments to the EHC Plan, despite having the capacity to choose these.

Thus, is there a pragmatic and legally acceptable solution that reduces the likelihood a young person will be deemed to lack capacity because they are unable to show an awareness of the abstract concept of the local authority? The MCA COP (3.9) states that it cannot stipulate exactly what information will be relevant in each case. It advises that someone helping a young person make a decision should follow the steps it sets out; these are guidance about presenting information. It helpfully recommends not giving too much detail, as it may confuse the young person, suggesting that in some cases broad information will suffice, provided it does not miss out important facts. The author believes this enables the pragmatic approach, set out below, to decide whether it is necessary to include an awareness of the local authority as part of the relevant information.

## Pragmatic approach for decisions related to the EHC Plan education sections

The sections of an EHC Plan are set out in the SEND COP (9.69).

Table 4.1 Summary of the education-related sections of an EHC Plan and the need for the young person to be aware of the local authority as part of considering their capacity

| EHC Plan Section | | Does the young person need to demonstrate an awareness of the local authority? |
|---|---|---|
| A | Views, interests and aspirations | No |
| B | Identified special educational needs | Yes |
| E | Outcomes | Possibly |
| F | Special educational provision | Yes |
| I | Educational placement | Yes |
| J | Personal budget | Yes |

This analysis suggests that there are circumstances when the young person will need to show an awareness that having their choice depends on the agreement of the local authority.

Section A is the young person's own views and aspirations, and as such, any suggested amendments are unlikely to be rejected by the local authority; therefore any decisions about this section could be considered without the need for the young person to indicate an awareness of the local authority.

Section B is about the identification of the young person's special needs. If the young person, or if they lack capacity to consider the matter, their parent, disagrees with the local authority about the content of this, they can appeal to the Tribunal, which is a legal process. Educational establishment staff will need to explain to the young person that the local authority will only consider proposed amendments, additions or deletions, to this section if they are supported in a report from a professional, such as a teacher/tutor, speech and language therapist, physiotherapist, occupational therapist or psychologist, healthcare professional or social worker or other professional. Generally, the report would have been shared as part of the annual review process. Therefore, any suggestions about changes to this section would require the young person to indicate they are aware the local authority has to agree their proposals. Alternatively, it may be that the young person does not wish to have something included that others at the annual review meeting think should be. Again, the young person would need to be considered to have the capacity to make this decision. If they do have the capacity, their decision should be respected.

Section E sets out the outcomes for the young person. This book is focused on education, so only educational outcomes are being considered here. Disagreements about the content of this section are not resolved at the Tribunal; nevertheless, an outcome can only be included if the local authority agrees. The emphasis on person-centred planning and involvement of the young person suggests that a young person could be working towards an outcome that may not be set out in their EHC Plan. If the young person chooses an outcome, and the provision needed to facilitate this being achieved is readily available without the need for it to be written into the EHC Plan, then the young person would not be required to demonstrate an awareness of the local authority or its agreement. On the other hand, if the outcome can only be achieved with provision that has to be set out in the EHC Plan, then the young person would have to indicate they know that the chosen outcome will only be part of their programme if the local authority agrees.

Section F details the special educational provision required to achieve the outcomes. Whilst disagreements about the outcomes (Section E) cannot be resolved at the Tribunal, Section F disputes can be appealed by the young person, or if they lack the capacity to do so, their parents. Therefore, it is advisable to consider the young person's awareness of the local authority's role in agreeing their chosen amendments.

Section I names the educational placement the young person should attend. This is wholly controlled by the local authority.

Therefore, the local authority's role in agreeing educational placements is definitely part of the relevant information. The young person will need to show an awareness that attending their chosen educational establishment is dependent on the local authority's agreement.

Section J is about personal budgets for education, health and social care. This book relates to education, so only this aspect of direct payments is considered here. The local authority may have information and resources for young people about this that can be used by educational establishment staff and parents to explain it to young people. However, given its complex and legalistic nature, it would be inappropriate to delegate a judgement about the young person's capacity to manage a personal budget to school or college staff. Only the relevant local authority officer can determine whether the young person has sufficient understanding to be allocated a personal budget. Nevertheless, it is strongly recommended that the local authority officer works collaboratively with educational establishment staff to ensure the MCA Principle 2 (all the help and support) is upheld.

### Explaining the concept of the local authority

The challenge is how to explain an abstract concept in a way that a young person with SEN will understand. If the young person has met the local authority officer managing their EHC Plan there may be a temptation to explain that Ms or Mr X has to agree this decision. Personifying the notion of 'local authority' may help the young person's understanding of the situation, but how will it affect a future working relationship if the local authority officer rejects the young person's choice? On the other hand, expecting young people to comprehend the abstract idea of the 'local authority' will place many at a disadvantage. Considering this dilemma in relation to the MCA Principle 2, giving young people all the help and support they need to make a decision, resolves it. The local authority ought to be represented recognisably with a face and name or logo. There is an argument for having an object of reference rather than the actual person, as the local authority officer may change caseloads or leave.

The difficulty utilising an inanimate object is that the young person may be aware that it cannot make decisions. So ideally, the local authority officer would agree to be photographed or recorded (for visually impaired young people) so the young person can put a face and/or voice to the name to assist their understanding.

Alternatively, local authority officers may have other suggestions as to how to represent the local authority in a way that can be understood. For example, all the SEN caseworkers may agree that the senior officer will represent the local authority, and this person's photograph is distributed to educational establishments as the embodiment of the local authority. Some young people will be accustomed to wearing a school uniform with a symbol representing the school, so they may be able to understand the council logo, used on all documents including their EHC Plan, as embodying the local authority. It is probably advisable to consult with educational establishment staff about the best way for the local authority to be represented for each young person.

### 2. Can the young person retain this information long enough to make the decision?

The MCA COP (4.20) states that people who can only hold information for a short time should not be assumed to lack capacity to decide. This guidance was probably written with people with dementia in mind. To reiterate, this is not an exam or a test – the young person can have all the help and support needed to facilitate them in making a decision. This includes having all the visual information they need in front of them, and verbal information repeated as often as necessary.

If there is a concern that the young person may not have retained information to make the decision, then the capacity assessment should be repeated a few days later. Assuming the young person makes the same choice, then it can be considered reliable. If the young person chooses a different option, this would raise questions about their ability to make the decision.

3. **Can the young person use and weigh the information to arrive at a choice?**

In the form expressed here, it would seem to be very challenging for many young people with SEN. However, analysing it seems to suggest that it is about the young person being able to indicate what they think is good, or not so good, or what they like, or dislike, about any of the options. Facilitating this is highly dependent on the assessor's skills at eliciting young people's views. As noted above, the young person has to achieve all the elements of the capacity assessment to be considered to have capacity. Therefore, it is essential that the assessor is trained and/or experienced in talking with young people with SEN, and is proficient in using a variety of communication strategies. This again raises the question of the local authority officer's skills and experience of talking with young people with SEN.

There is a range of strategies that may assist a young person to achieve this element of a capacity assessment. Using a visual process, for example, a Talking Mat™ style approach, would probably be most helpful, so the young person and the assessor can see the young person's views. Photographing this would maintain a record of the young person's opinions, which could assist demonstrating that the young person does have capacity, or enable a comparison to be made, if a capacity assessment has to be repeated, due to concerns about its reliability. A photographic record could be an important source of information for parents making a 'best interests' decision on behalf of their young person, assuming the young person is considered to lack capacity to make this particular decision.

In relation to decisions requiring consideration of the local authority's role, it is important to carefully ascertain the young person's understanding, as this may be the difference between being considered to have, or lack, capacity. The SEND COP emphasises young people's involvement in decision-making about their education. Therefore, it is hoped that, over the years the young person been the subject of an EHC Plan, they may have been made aware that suggested amendments have to be approved by the local authority. Ideally, the young person will have been introduced to an embodiment of the local authority and adopted one they understand. Hence, by the time a young person reaches the age where they are allowed to make their own decision, they may have an awareness of the local authority and its role, as well as having their favoured representation. When undertaking a capacity assessment, the assessor should know the young person's preferred representation and have it available.

What constitutes an acceptable understanding of the local authority's role? The young person's comprehension of the information only has to be at a basic level, not all the nuances. Therefore, if the young person can demonstrate that they know the local authority will say 'yes' or 'no' to the suggested amendments, and that 'yes' means it will happen, and 'no' that it will not, this is sufficient.

> Jill is 17 years old with Down's syndrome and attends her local special school. She communicates using Makaton signing and saying some single words. She enjoys using her iPad to take photos, play games, and to assist her communication.
>
> Jill has to decide if she wants to remain in her current school for another year, or transfer to the local FE college for a life skills course. She has been attending the FE college for a day a week for the past year with other students and staff from her current school. In preparation for making the decision, the school staff have been talking with Jill, as well as assisting her to use her iPad to take photos of key staff and relevant places in college and school. School staff have used Jill's iPad to make some videos of her doing various activities in both settings. In addition, Jill has recorded her college tutor and school class teacher explaining and showing her what will be offered assuming she attended that educational establishment.
>
> As Jill's choice has to be agreed by the local authority, school staff have been introducing the concept and finding a representation Jill can understand. Jill's tutors, Mrs Jacobs and Mr Singh, had a problem-solving session

## 'More Serious or Significant Decisions'

to come up with possible ways that Jill may understand the notion of the local authority. Jill likes cats. Mr Singh recalled that when Ms Joseph, the local authority SEN officer managing Jill's EHC Plan, attended the last annual review meeting, she had a cat-shaped brooch that Jill liked. Perhaps either a photo of Ms Joseph or the brooch could be a possibility? Jill likes all animals. The city's coat of arms, on all council correspondence, including Jill's EHC Plan, has owls – would an owl be an option? Jill has visited the council offices – perhaps a photo of the building should be considered?

Following the meeting, Mr Singh contacted Ms Joseph to request a photo of her with her cat brooch and just the brooch. Mrs Jacobs cut out the council's coat of arms from an EHC Plan and mounted it on card; she did the same with a photo of the council offices.

Mrs Jacobs meets with Jill to try out the various possible representations of the local authority. She shows Jill the photo of Ms Joseph and her cat brooch. Jill remembers the brooch, but not Ms Joseph, or that she works for the local authority. Jill recognises her EHC Plan. Mrs Jacobs gives Jill the council's coat of arms; however, Jill does not recognise it as something she has seen on her EHC Plan. Mrs Jacobs points out the coat of arms on the EHC Plan; Jill does not seem interested. Finally, Mrs Jacobs presents the photo of the council offices; again, Jill shows no recognition. Mrs Jacobs reminds Jill that this is where she met the mayor last year. Jill does not seem to have any recollection. Mrs Jacobs had an idea – as Jill recognises her EHC Plan and Ms Joseph's cat brooch, perhaps a photo of Ms Joseph, with her cat brooch, holding Jill's EHC Plan may be a good way of representing the local authority's role?

Mrs Jacobs emails Ms Joseph to request a photo of her with her cat brooch, holding Jill's EHC Plan. Ms Joseph again obliges. Mrs Jacobs shows Jill the new photo on her iPad. Jill recognises her EHC Plan and the cat brooch; she finds the photo amusing. Mrs Jacobs

109

believes this is probably the best way to represent the local authority for Jill.

---

**4. Can the young person communicate the decision in any way?**

The young person can use any verbal or non-verbal means of communicating their choice. The onus is on the assessor to be sure that they can understand the young person's means of communication.

## *Does the young person have capacity to make this decision?*

> **Recap**
> - Capacity is either *Yes* or *No*; there is no such thing as partial capacity.
> - If the answer to *one or more* of the 'four key questions' is *No* then, on the balance of probabilities, the young person lacks capacity to make this decision at this time.

The MCA COP (4.48) explains that in borderline cases, or where there is doubt, the assessor must be able to show that it is more likely than not that the answer to any of the four questions is 'no'.

A reminder – this is only for this decision at this time; the young person may be able to make other decisions. However, even if the young person lacked capacity for this decision at this time, they may be able to make a similar decision in the future, particularly if making decisions has been an outcome in a person-centred plan or EHC Plan.

## Does a young person's capacity have to be assessed for every 'more serious or significant' or 'legal consequences' decision?

The SEND COP Annex 1 notes that, if there is doubt about a young person's mental capacity, consideration needs to be given as to whether the person lacks capacity. It goes on to state that:

> this does not necessarily mean that a person's capacity has to be reassessed each time a decision needs to be taken. If there is a reasonable belief the person lacks capacity to make a decision based on prior knowledge of that person, the decision can be made by a parent or representative as appropriate. (SEND COP, p.274)

By now the reader should be aware that this statement is incorrect and misleading, as it contravenes the primary MCA principle, presumption of capacity, and the MCA Principle 2, all the help and support to make a decision. Following the SEND COP advice is likely to lead to a young person being denied the opportunity to make their own decision. A young person, their parents or representative, or another professional, can challenge conclusions about the young person having, or lacking, capacity. In this case, if the matter cannot be resolved through a local dispute resolution process, it can lead to an independent body, such as the Court of Protection, being asked to determine the matter. An education professional risks criticism if they are unable to demonstrate they have followed the MCA COP. Generally, a young person's capacity to make a particular decision needs to be considered for every 'more serious or significant' or 'legal consequences' decision.

The author can hear the comments that surely the SEND COP Annex 1 is being pragmatic, as professionals cite the example of a young person with profound and multiple learning difficulties, functioning at a very young age, with no meaningful verbal communication. Undoubtedly, this young person would be found to lack capacity for many 'more serious and significant' and 'legal consequences' decisions, and it would be fruitless to assess this repeatedly. The MCA COP (4.28–4.29) acknowledges that some young people may have an 'ongoing condition that condition that affects their ability to make certain decisions' (p.50), but states 'it is important to review capacity from time to time, as people can improve their decision-making capabilities' (p.50). Thus, for a very limited group of young people, it may be appropriate to base a conclusion about a young person's capacity to make the decision on prior knowledge. However, the onus is on the education professional, using their prior knowledge, to ensure they can justify this. It would be advisable, and good practice, to keep a record of the reasons that, on the balance of probabilities, the young person lacks capacity to make the specific decision.

## Summary

- Not all young people receiving support under the SEND COP or who are the subject of an EHC plan will meet the capacity assessment Stage 1 criteria for it to be considered that they may lack capacity to make the decision.

- A capacity assessment is a two-stage process that answers the two questions set out in the MCA COP Chapter 4.

- The Stage 1 question of a capacity assessment establishes if the young person meets the criteria to be considered to possibly lack capacity for the particular decision.

- The Stage 2 question is answered using the 'four key questions' that form the basis of a capacity assessment.

- A capacity assessment is not a test or exam – it is an enabling process.

- A capacity assessment is confidential.

- In keeping with the MCA Principle 2, the young person should have all the help and support they require to assist them making the decision.

- Generally, a young person's capacity should be considered for every 'more serious or significant' or 'legal consequences' decision.

- The outcome of a capacity assessment is that, on the balance of probabilities, the young person has, or lacks, capacity for this decision, at this time.

- The SEND COP Annex 1 is incorrect and misleading as it:
    - omits Stage 1 of a capacity assessment
    - does not set out the two questions to be answered
    - only includes the 'four key questions' that form the basis of a capacity assessment
    - advises that capacity does not have to be reassessed for every decision, and if there is a reasonable belief the young person lacks capacity based on prior knowledge, their parent or representative can make the decision.

- The person who requires the decision-making is the person who assesses a young person's capacity to make the choice. Thus, it will be different people for different decisions.

- Any education professional assessing a young person's capacity needs to be trained in the MCA principles and in undertaking a capacity assessment.

- The person undertaking the assessment is known as the assessor.

- Local authority officers, with minimal training and experience of working with young people with SEN, will need to work with educational establishment staff to determine a young person's capacity for the particular decision.

- The assessor needs to:

- know the young person, how they function, their preferred format for information, and their language comprehension ability, as well as understanding the young person's communication style
- be aware of and consider any factors affecting a young person's decision-making performance, such as attention and concentration issues, the effects of medical conditions or medication on functioning, or cultural considerations
- consider other barriers to decision-making, such as being concerned about making the wrong choice
- think about how to plan and carry out a capacity assessment, taking into consideration where, for example, an appropriate location; when, a time of day when the young person is most alert; and how, including any equipment or resources needed
- know the relevant information for the particular decision
- know the young person's preferred representation of the local authority
- record the capacity assessment, ideally on a capacity assessment record form.

• Some decisions related to an EHC Plan require the young person to show an awareness of the abstract concept of the local authority.

• For a very limited group of young people, such as those with profound and multiple learning difficulties, it may be appropriate to use prior knowledge to determine their capacity to make a particular 'more serious or significant' or 'legal consequences' decision.

*Chapter 5*

# 'Legal Consequences' Decisions
## Appealing to the SEND Tribunal

> **Recap**
> - For it to be considered a young person may lack capacity, it *must* be shown that they meet the capacity assessment Stage 1 criteria (see Chapter 4).
> - Not all young people receiving support under the SEND COP, or who are the subject of an EHC Plan, meet the capacity assessment Stage 1 criteria for it to be considered they may lack capacity to make the particular decision.

This chapter, which *should be read* in conjunction with Chapter 4, explores the relevant information and key concepts specifically related to appealing (bringing an appeal) to the Special Educational Needs and Disability (SEND) Tribunal (the Tribunal). This forms the basis of a capacity assessment ascertaining whether the young person has the capacity to bring an appeal. As noted in Chapter 4, the young person has to demonstrate a basic understanding of the relevant information, or key concepts, not the fine details or nuances.

It is essential that the assessor is familiar with the relevant information, an important part being the Tribunal process.[1] The assessor may find it beneficial to discuss being at the hearing with an education professional who has attended one.

The Children and Families Act 2014 gives young people the right to make particular decisions about Education, Health and Care

---

1   A guide to the Tribunal is available at www.gov.uk/special-educational-needs-disability-tribunal/overview.

(EHC) Plans from the end of Year 11 (Y11), provided they have the capacity (Special Educational Needs and Disability Code of Practice (SEND COP) 8.15–8.16, 8.21). If the young person disagrees with the local authority about these matters, they have the right to appeal to the Tribunal, subject to their capacity to do so (SEND COP 11.44). Despite being termed a 'young person', adulthood begins on their 18th birthday, so from then it is assumed a young person will bring their own appeals, unless it is proved they are unable to do so (Mental Capacity Act 2005 Code of Practice (MCA COP) 2.3). This means the young person signs the form that registers the appeal (Application for Appeal, Young person aged 16–25 years form, SEND24A[2]) with the Tribunal.

The MCA COP (4.10) states that anybody claiming the young person lacks capacity to make the decision must be able to provide proof. They need to able to show that, on the balance of probabilities, it is more likely than not that the young person lacks capacity to make this particular decision. If a legal representative has signed the Application for Appeal form, the young person's capacity to bring the appeal cannot be questioned.

The SEND COP (11.45) sets out the issues that a young person can appeal to the Tribunal. These are:

- decision by a local authority not to carry out an education, health and care needs assessment or re-assessment

- decision by a local authority not to issue an EHC Plan following an assessment

- description of the young person's special educational needs (SEN) specified in Section B of the EHC Plan

- special educational provision specified in Section F

- type and name of the educational establishment in Section I or that none is specified

---

2   This form is available at www.gov.uk/special-educational-needs-disability-tribunal/appeal-to-tribunal.

- amendment to Sections B, F or I of the EHC Plan
- decision by a local authority not to amend an EHC Plan following a review or re-assessment
- decision by a local authority to cease to maintain an EHC Plan.

## Capacity to bring an appeal

Bringing an appeal to the Tribunal, in effect, involves the young person being able to make two decisions that are separated in time. The time lag between making the choice and knowing that the local authority disagrees with this is from about one to four months. The delay relates to various statutory time limits that apply to certain decisions, such as asking for an assessment, awaiting the local authority's decision about making an EHC Plan, requesting an amendment to an EHC Plan following a review or re-assessment, or choosing a new educational placement at a phase transfer. The Mental Capacity Act (MCA) 2005 emphasises that a person may be able to make one decision at the time it is needed, but not another. Nevertheless, in this case, the decision to bring an appeal is linked to the choices the young person made in relation to their EHC Plan or to request one, some time ago. Hence, to be considered to have capacity to bring an appeal, the young person has to demonstrate they know about the decision the local authority was considering and has not agreed, as well as the Tribunal process.

As noted in Chapter 4, the young person has to demonstrate an understanding of the local authority's role to be considered to have capacity to make decisions that could lead to a Tribunal. It was mooted that this may result in some young people who could understand the choice they wished to make being considered to lack capacity, as they were unable to demonstrate an awareness of the abstract idea of the local authority. Does this mean the young person had to have capacity to make the EHC Plan-related decision at the time it was needed, to be considered to have capacity to bring an appeal? Logically, the answer to this should be 'yes', but in the time elapsing, between making the decision and the outcome of the local authority's deliberations, this may have led to the young person having a better understanding of the choices and what they want. Other factors may have changed in the intervening time, such as improvements in the young person's mental health, emotional wellbeing or other health issues that impaired their ability to make the decision when it was required. Thus, the answer is, the young person did not necessarily have to have capacity to make the EHC Plan-related decision at the time it was needed. However, in relation to the capacity to bring an appeal, the young person must demonstrate an understanding of the choice they, or their parents or representative, made on their behalf.

Therefore, a capacity assessment to bring an appeal to the Tribunal can be considered to have two parts in relation to the young person understanding the relevant information: Part 1, a general understanding of the choices rejected by the local authority that have led to the appeal to the Tribunal; and Part 2, a basic understanding of the Tribunal process.

## Part 1: Relevant information and key concepts related to the decision that has given rise to the appeal

The concepts and information presented here are a guide. Possibly, there will be other information, very specific to the particular decision or related to local factors that the young person may need to show an awareness of. In all cases, the young person must show they know:

- that there was a decision
- what they, their parent or representative suggested as the preferred option
- that it is the local authority that decides whether to agree to their choice, in their role as managing (looking after) the EHC Plan
- what the local authority has chosen and why.

For example:

Jill attends her local special school. She has to decide if she wants to remain in her current school for another year, or transfer to one of the local FE colleges, Moor Park, or St Lucia College, for a life skills course. She has been attending Moor Park a day a week for the past year with other students and staff from her current school. In early January, she chose Moor Park on the local authority college preference form. School staff and her parents agreed Jill had the capacity to make this decision. When Jill received her amended EHC Plan on 31 March, the local authority had named St Lucia College in Part I. The local authority explained their choice in the letter. They had chosen St Lucia as it was nearer to Jill's home, and this would make developing her ability to travel independently more likely than for a college further away. She had been allocated shared minibus transport until she was able to travel independently. Jill knows there is a bus from the main road near her home to St Lucia College. She used the bus with her mother to travel to the college, as part of the decision-making process. It had been explained to Jill that the local authority like young people to learn to travel independently to college.

When talking with Jill, it is expected that she would be able to demonstrate she knows that:

- o she had chosen Moor Park

- o the local authority has said she has to attend St Lucia College

- o the local authority looks after the EHC Plan and it is they who say what happens

- o the local authority has chosen St Lucia College because it is closer to her home

- o the local authority thinks it will be easier for Jill to learn to travel independently

- there is a bus from near her home to St Lucia College
- the same bus goes to Moor Park after it has passed St Lucia College.

The outcome of an annual review meeting may propose several amendments to an EHC Plan, but the local authority may accept some. This raises the question about whether the young person needs to know about every change they wanted that has not been agreed. An appeal is about all the areas of the EHC Plan that are in dispute, so logically, the young person does need to show a broad general awareness of all the areas of dispute to be considered to have capacity to bring the appeal. Like many aspects of applying the MCA, this may seem harsh, if the young person is aware of the majority of disputed amendments.

The MCA has built in safeguards in terms of the 'best interests' checklist, which states that the young person's parents should take account of the young person's wishes and feelings when making a decision on their behalf. Furthermore, the Tribunal requests that the young person's views are presented. Additionally, the young person can attend the hearing. This may be sitting through the whole hearing, or talking with the panel beforehand, to ascertain the young person's wishes and feelings.

1. **Decision by a local authority not to carry out an education, health and care needs assessment or re-assessment**

The basic key points the young person will probably need to demonstrate are:

- they need some help with their learning or school/college work
- the local authority was asked to look at what help is needed to assist with learning or school/college work

- the local authority has said it does not need to look at the help, as the young person can get all the help they need from the school/college.

2. **Decision by a local authority not to issue an EHC Plan following an assessment**

The basic key points the young person will probably need to demonstrate are:

- they need some help with their learning or school/college work
- the local authority has looked at what help is needed to assist with learning or school/college work
- the local authority has said that all the help that is needed is already in place at school/college and it does not need to give anything extra, or
- the school/college is the right one to give the help that is needed.

3. **The description of the young person's SEN specified in Section B of the EHC Plan**

The basic key points the young person will probably need to demonstrate are:

- in general terms, they wanted something(s) added or removed about their SEN, and some indication they are aware to what this related
- the addition or removal had to be supported by a professional's report
- the local authority had not agreed to the change
- the local authority's reason for not amending the EHC Plan in the way the young person wished.

122   For example:

> Jill has Down's syndrome and a bilateral sensori-neural hearing loss, which has recently deteriorated. The hearing loss in her right ear was mild; it is now moderate. Her hearing aids have had to be reprogrammed to accommodate this change. Her eyesight has also changed and she has new glasses. Jill's EHC Plan in Section B records her hearing loss as it was a year ago, and notes that she wears glasses. Jill wants it changed to reflect the deterioration in both her vision and hearing. Her proposed amendments are, 'Her hearing loss has got worse in the right ear and is now a moderate hearing loss' and 'Her eyesight has got worse and she has had to have new glasses'. The report from the Teacher of the Deaf records the change in hearing, but there is no professional report noting the extent of her changed vision, and how this will have an impact on her access to education. The new EHC Plan is issued including the amendment in relation to her hearing, but not her vision. The local authority explains that this is because there was no professional report, such as from an optician or hospital consultant, which states there has been a significant change in her vision and how this affects her learning.
>
> In this case, Jill would need to show that it was information about her vision that she wished to have added – in broad terms, that it has got worse. She will also have to have some awareness that it needs to be written in a professional report and that this needs to be sent to the local authority. Additionally, she will have to show that she knows the local authority looks after the EHC Plan, and decides whether to agree a suggested amendment.

### 4. The special educational provision specified in Section F

The basic key points the young person will probably need to demonstrate are:

- they wanted something added or removed about the help they receive or activities they engage in. They would have to show a broad idea about what this related to, for example, when or how they receive support, for what areas of the curriculum, or an activity such as horse riding or work experience

- the local authority has not agreed to make the amendment in their role as looking after the EHC Plan

- the reason(s) the local authority has given for not making the desired change(s).

5. **The type and name of the educational establishment in Section I, or that there is none specified**

The basic key points the young person will probably need to demonstrate are:

- which educational establishment they chose

- why they chose this establishment

- which educational establishment has been named in the EHC Plan

- who decided that they should attend this establishment

- why it has been decided that they should attend this establishment

- why, in general terms, the local authority is saying they do not agree to naming the young person's choice of establishment in the EHC Plan.

6. **A decision by a local authority not to amend an EHC Plan following a review or re-assessment**

The basic key points the young person will probably need to demonstrate are:

- they wanted something(s) added or removed about their SEN, and some indication they are aware to what this related
- the addition or removal had to be supported by a professional's report
- the local authority had not agreed to the change in their role as managing the EHC Plan
- the local authority's reason for not amending the EHC Plan in the way the young person wished.

7. **A decision by a local authority to cease to maintain an EHC Plan**

The basic key points the young person will probably need to demonstrate are:

- they have an EHC Plan
- the local authority manage this
- the local authority want to stop looking after the EHC Plan
- the reason the local authority want to stop doing this
- why the young person disagrees with the local authority no longer looking after the EHC Plan.

## Part 2: Relevant information and key concepts related to the Tribunal process

Although the Tribunal is part of Her Majesty's Courts and Tribunals Service, it is extremely rare for witnesses to be asked to formally swear the oath. It is taken on trust that all parties will provide truthful information.

The young person will have to show in general terms:

- they understand the concept of the Tribunal
- an awareness of the process

- what they will have to do in relation to the specific issue(s) they are asking the Tribunal to decide.

## 1. The concept of the Tribunal

The young person will have to show in general terms that they are aware:

- the Tribunal is independent of the local authority
- the panel has a judge
- what a judge is
- the panel will have one or two other people as well as the judge who know about EHC Plans
- the Tribunal panel will make the decision about the matters it is being asked to consider
- the decision of the Tribunal is binding on all parties.

## 2. The Tribunal process

The young person will have to show in general terms that they are aware:

- who the Tribunal panel should listen to (both sides)
- who they can have with them in the hearing (witnesses, someone to support them such as their parent, other relative or friend and/or a representative)
- who else will be at the hearing (the local authority and its witnesses)
- they are likely to need help preparing for the Tribunal and/or in the hearing
- they can identify who could help them and/or how to access support

- that going to the Tribunal does not guarantee that the Tribunal panel will choose to agree to the young person's choices.

3. **What they will have to do in relation to the specific issue(s) they are asking the Tribunal to decide**

In very general terms, the young person will need to show they know:

- they need reports from the relevant professional(s) and/or that professional(s) to attend the hearing as a witness to give information orally. Who this is will depend on the issue. For example, if a young person wants something about their speech and language skills in Sections B and/or F, they will need a report from a speech and language therapist, and possibly, that speech and language therapist may need to attend the hearing

- they will need someone from their current educational establishment to write a report and/or attend the hearing to give information.

If the appeal is about which educational establishment the young person wants named in Section I, the young person will need to demonstrate they know that:

- their chosen establishment has to have stated, in writing, that there is a place for them

- the establishment will or has provided a report, setting out how it will meet the provision in the EHC Plan, or that someone from the establishment will attend the hearing to give information.

## Summary

This chapter should be read in conjunction with Chapter 4 in this book.

- Children and Families Act 2014 gives young people the right to make decisions about their EHC Plan from the end of Y11 (after the last Friday in June).

- The SEND COP (11.45) sets out the issues a young person can appeal to the Tribunal, provided they have the capacity to do so.

- The assessor needs to be familiar with the Tribunal process.

- For a young person to appeal to the Tribunal, they have to understand two decisions separated in time: the decision about the content of the EHC Plan, and the decision to appeal to the Tribunal.

- To be considered to have capacity to appeal to the Tribunal the young person needs to demonstrate they understand the concept of the Tribunal, show an awareness of the Tribunal process and what they have to do in relation to the particular issue they wish to appeal.

*Chapter 6*

# Additional Considerations for Educational Psychologists

> This chapter should be read in conjunction with Chapter 4.

Prior to the implementation of the Mental Capacity Act (MCA) 2005 in 2007, the British Psychological Society (BPS) envisaged that the main group of psychologists working with the MCA would be clinical psychologists. In 2006, the BPS published interim guidance about assessing mental capacity for clinical psychologists. This remains in place, and has not been amended, although it was intended it would be developed over time to reflect how the legislation was being used in routine clinical practice. Since it is the only professional guidance available, educational psychologists (EPs) would be advised to read it, although it is not wholly relevant to an EP's role and way of working. Nevertheless, it does raise some important issues and considerations.

In 2010, the BPS, in conjunction with the Social Care Institute for Excellence (SCIE), published an audit tool for mental capacity assessments that aimed to set standards, and guide and improve practice for individual practitioners, as well as organisations. Originally devised for clinical psychologists, it is considered appropriate for other professionals such as speech and language therapists. Despite having a focus on health and social care settings, much of it is applicable to EPs, to facilitate reflection on their own assessments, as well as use at service level to develop policy and practice.

The BPS and Royal College of Psychiatrists (2007) jointly produced a leaflet giving a brief overview of the main points of the legislation, with some advice about what assessments may be used. This is a much better summary of the MCA than the Special Educational Needs and Disability Code of Practice (SEND COP) Annex 1, as it includes the full criteria to be considered 'to lack capacity', as well as being explicit about the functional approach.

Since 2007, much has been written about the MCA for doctors, social workers and nurses, including exploring how these professionals have incorporated this into their clinical practice (Walji, Fletcher and Weatherhead 2014), but very little for, or about, clinical psychologists. Walji et al. (2014) report what they consider to be the only published study exploring the experiences of clinical psychologists, albeit a small-scale study. Whilst clinical psychologists' practice is different from EPs', their views about working with the MCA are likely to have some relevance to EPs, providing a stimulus for discussion and reflection on practice.

Fox (2015) discusses EP practice and developing a child or young person's autonomy in relation to the Children and Families Act 2014 principles. Despite the chosen case study focusing on a ten-year-old child, Fox's thought-provoking exploration of the issues is very relevant to the post-16 age range, thereby providing another perspective for EP's to consider in relation to their application of the MCA principles. His discussion centres on the moral principles that may now underpin the work of EPs and includes discussions about autonomy, position theory, paternalism, beneficence and social justice, as well as reflection on 'what sort of person should an EP be?' (p.394).

## An educational psychologist's role in assessing a young person's capacity in relation to educational decisions

This discussion focuses on the EP's role in relation to their responsibilities under the Children and Families Act 2014 assessing a young person's capacity to make educational decisions. As noted in Chapter 4, the person who assesses the young person's capacity to make a decision is usually the person who needs the decision to be made (Mental Capacity Act 2005 Code of Practice (MCA COP)

4.38). Generally, this will be educational establishment staff or local authority SEN officers. Occasionally it may be an EP, if direct work with the EP is being offered to the young person; in many ways, this is a formalisation of the familiar practice of obtaining informed consent. The MCA COP (4.42 and 4.51) indicates the assessor may need another professional's opinion about the young person's capacity to make a particular decision and lists psychologists, without an indication of particular specialism, as another possible professional who could be consulted. Thus, it is clear that the EP's role in assessing capacity is advisory to the person who needs the decision. This advisory role carries a heavy weight of responsibility, which was something that concerned the clinical psychologists in Walji et al's (2014) study, and undoubtedly EPs will be able to relate to this.

The MCA COP (4.52) clearly states that a professional's opinion must be based on a proper assessment of the young person's capacity to make the decision. It indicates that this is a process that takes time. The MCA (4.61) highlights the need to keep relevant professional records. As already noted in previous chapters, it is good practice to use a capacity assessment record form (see, for example, Appendix 1).

The BPS (2006) guidance and MCA COP (4.53) suggest an applied psychologist's assessment may be requested when there is disagreement between professionals and parents, or carers, or differences of opinions between other professionals, about a young person's capacity. It raises the issue of the applied psychologist being placed in a situation where there are strong emotions. This situation is very familiar to EPs as they often mediate between parents and education professionals.

The clear status of the EP's advisory role can be viewed as helpful as it will enable conversations with the assessor, the young person and their parents. It also facilitates joint working with the assessor to arrive at a shared decision. The MCA COP (4.51) notes, that for some young people, a multi-disciplinary approach is beneficial. The BPS (2006) guidance advocates applied psychologists sharing assessments and decision-making with colleagues from other disciplines. Walji et al. (2014) reported this approach was highly valued by the clinical psychologists. This is established practice for EPs.

The Children and Families Act 2014 applies to young people in the youth justice system, but this chapter does not explore the issue of capacity related to youth offending or the criminal justice system. EPs can find information relating to assessing a young person's capacity for matters such as ability to stand trial or to be a witness in the BPS (2006) guidance.

However, EPs may be asked to advise about a young person's capacity to bring an appeal to the Special Educational Needs and Disability (SEND) Tribunal, if someone is concerned about their capacity to do so. Chapter 5 addresses capacity assessments for the SEND Tribunal, assuming the young person is bringing the appeal in their own right, that is, they signed the form to register the appeal. However, a young person's capacity does not need to be considered if their parents have brought the appeal, that is, signed the form to register the appeal, if it is clear this is with the young person's consent.

As young people may be attending educational establishments up to 25 years old, it is possible that EPs may be asked to advise about a young person's capacity to consent to sexual relations or marriage, which are excluded from the MCA as issues another person can decide on behalf of the young person who lacks capacity (MCA COP 1.10). The BPS (2006) guidance covers capacity to consent to sexual relations in some depth. Sexual intercourse is illegal with a young person who does not understand the 'nature of the act' or 'reasonably foreseeable consequences' (BPS 2006). Additionally, since June 2014, as noted in Chapter 4, forced marriage has become a criminal offence in England and Wales.

The SEND COP Annex 1 states that it is the young person's parent or representative who will make the decision if the young person lacks the capacity to do so. Therefore, unlike clinical psychologists, EPs will not routinely play a part in 'best interests' decisions. However, as noted in Chapter 4, when making the decision parents should use information recorded during a capacity assessment relating to a young person's views, wishes and feelings. Possibly parents may wish to meet with those who have undertaken the capacity assessment to assist them making the decision. However, if there is a concern by an education professional that the parental choice is not in the young person's 'best interests', then the EP who assisted an assessor with the capacity assessment would be invited to attend a meeting with the parents to discuss the matter (see Chapter 8).

## Considerations for educational psychologists

Walji et al. (2014) interviewed seven clinical psychologists about their experiences of implementing the MCA since 2007. Whilst acknowledging this small sample may not be representative of the whole profession, common themes did emerge. General comments about the implementation of MCA in healthcare settings, both from the psychologists' and service users' (young persons') perspectives, as well as issues raised, are pertinent to EPs and EP services.

### *Understanding the MCA, training and access to information*

Walji et al. (2014) noted that service users and their carers expressed concerns about professionals' commitment to the fundamental principle of assumed capacity. The clinical psychologists in the study reported a good understanding of the MCA, and some of the issues raised indicated the ethical dilemma adhering to the principle of the presumption of capacity. On the other hand, they noted that some aspects of the MCA are unclear, and reported uncertainties about the proper implementation of some MCA processes, citing 'best interests' as a particularly contentious issue. They attributed disagreements with professionals from other disciplines as to a person's capacity as due to differences in understanding or interpretation of the MCA. Overall, the clinical psychologists felt it was very important to follow the correct procedures. This accords with the BPS (2006) guidance advising applied psychologists to have regard to the legal framework when conducting assessments and to ensure they uphold the MCA principles.

The clinical psychologists highlighted the importance of adequate training, but felt that too much of what they had received focused on the legislation rather than the clinical assessment of capacity. They considered the case examples given were too specific and hard to relate to their own client group. This was raised as an issue for education professionals in Chapter 2 in relation to the lack of relevance of the MCA COP case study examples; it is interesting that some clinical psychologists also find them unhelpful. The clinical psychologists noted they learned the most through their clinical practice, as well as valuing appropriate supervision and peer support. They also wanted books, journal articles or other resources focusing on practical matters.

At the time of undertaking the study, Walji was a trainee clinical psychologist. She noted that MCA work is not included in doctoral training, and advocated that it should be. This was most surprising. However, it is unlikely to be the case for EP training, as the survey by Atkinson, Dunsmuir, Lang and Wright (2015) shows that 95% of EP respondents thought that including the MCA in the initial training curriculum for EPs was either extremely important or important. Atkinson *et al.* (2015) have included the MCA in their proposed competency framework for trainee EPs working with young people aged 16–25. They also suggest this framework could be used by EP services, at both service and individual practitioner level, to assist in developing practice to work with this age group.

The Walji *et al.* (2014) study was undertaken prior to the Supreme Court judgment in March 2014 giving a new definition of deprivation of liberty, and the subsequent Law Society guidance (2015) on the matter.

The BPS guidance (2006) and the clinical psychologists' actual experience suggests EPs would benefit from training and resources that:

- ensure an understanding of the MCA principles
- have a practical focus on undertaking capacity assessments, including assessment approaches

- discuss the implications of a capacity assessment in relation to the young person and their parents

- present relevant education-focused case studies

- enable appropriate supervision

- facilitate a shared understanding of the MCA with other education professionals

- provide an awareness of 'best interests'

- explore the implication of the Law Society guidance on deprivation of liberty for EP practice, including safeguarding responsibilities.

## *Ethical and professional issues*

The BPS (2006) guidance states there should be high standards of professional practice. It notes the importance of objective assessments, separating out factual information from interpretation, and a clearly stated rationale for the conclusion.

Like most psychological assessments, there is a degree of subjectivity in interpreting the outcome of a capacity assessment. The BPS (2006) document raises the issue of the psychologist's personal views, which, if unacknowledged, may lead to biased conclusions. These include the psychologist's beliefs about the decision for which the assessment is required, as well as any strongly held views about the rights of particular groups of young people being enabled to make their own decisions, for example, those with learning difficulties. It was suggested that in the latter case the psychologist might find it difficult to conclude the young person lacks capacity to make the decision, and this may have far-reaching consequences. The BPS guidance suggests that a psychologist may adopt a defensive approach due to concerns about what may occur if things go wrong. For example, if the young person was considered to have the capacity to choose which college to attend, but when they actually transfer there, do not like it and become reluctant to go – what would happen then? In some instances it was proposed the psychologist may adopt an approach that confuses assessing a young person's capacity for the decision with considering what may be in their 'best interests'.

The clinical psychologists (Walji *et al.* 2014) highlighted possible conflicts with professional values that promote autonomy and individual choice. They were very aware that capacity, or lack of capacity, had an impact on personal freedoms and affected not only the individual, but also their family and carers.

Walji *et al.* (2014) reported that the clinical psychologists were very mindful of their professional responsibilities, highlighting the importance of not jumping to conclusions too quickly about an individual's capacity. They also stressed the need to be able to defend an assessment.

The clinical psychologists reflected on the incongruity of their usual practice of using formulation and the MCA being 'yes' or 'no'. As already noted, EPs are not the only education professionals who are likely to find this black and white approach discomfiting. Whilst underlining the negative aspects of implementing the MCA, the clinical psychologists referred to the positive effect on their practice in terms of identifying what constituted best practice to ensure assessments promoted and facilitated their client's decision-making abilities, as well as being rigorous.

Some reasons for a capacity assessment had far-reaching consequences for the client, such as having their children taken into care. The clinical psychologists discussed finding these situations difficult, and sought support from supervisors and colleagues.

## *Service guidance*

Within a year of the implementation of the MCA, a survey of neuropsychologists in 2008 (Todd *et al.* 2008, cited in Walji *et al.* 2014) reported concerns about the lack of specific practice guidelines, confidence in their assessment abilities, the usefulness of standardised neuropsychological tests, and ethical dilemmas relating to potential conflicts with professional values. Walji *et al.* (2014) noted that some NHS trusts have developed guidelines particularly for their service and client groups. Additionally, some individual practitioners have devised their own system.

EP services would be advised to:

- produce guidance for EPs

- provide information leaflets about the advisory nature of the EP, in relation to a capacity assessment, for educational establishment staff, local authority officers, young people and parents

- develop a service capacity assessment form (see Appendix 1) to record the young person's responses and EP's reasoning for the conclusion, which will assist the actual assessor in making their decision about the young person's capacity. Furthermore, it will show how the assessment was undertaken, should the outcome be questioned by the young person, their parents or anyone else involved with the decision

- provide support to an EP whose decision is being challenged

- have a process of peer support and/or supervision to enable a discussion of assessments and reports, as well as to reflect on personal value judgements, and any emotional impact on the psychologist of the outcome of the assessment (BPS 2006)

- encourage use of the BPS and SCIE audit tool (2010) to reflect on a capacity assessment and develop practice; Atkinson *et al.* (2015) also advocate the use of this

- ensure the service approach to capacity assessments forms a part of the induction of EPs and trainee EPs joining the service

- adopt Atkinson *et al.*'s (2015) competency framework to support developing the service and individual EP practice in this area.

## Assessment approaches and time

A young person's experiences of and views about an assessment are very important, as these may affect reliability and validity. Walji et al. (2014) reported that service users and their carers expressed concerns about the use of inappropriate assessment tools which were either unsuited to the individual, and/or the decision under consideration. As noted above, the neuropsychologists surveyed in 2008 had misgivings about their tests being suitable for assessing capacity. American neuropsychologists have also expressed concerns about the ecological validity of standardised assessments employed to assess real-life situations (Walji et al. 2014). There are no widely used standardised assessments of capacity; the BPS guidance (2006) proposes a practical framework (Walji et al. 2014), as well as ensuring the tests selected are relevant to the situation, and the psychologist is aware of reliability and validity issues.

EPs differ from clinical psychologists as they generally assess young people in their educational establishment, enabling observations of the young person's functioning in a natural setting, as well as the opportunity to triangulate information with staff. EPs use a range of qualitative and quantitative methods rather than predominantly relying on standardised tests/questionnaires. So concerns about the suitability of assessment tools may be less of an issue for EPs, but should not be ignored. Producing service guidance ought to be an opportunity to consider assessment approaches and materials that facilitate a young person's decision-making. Chapter 4 stressed the need to plan a capacity assessment in advance, which should include consideration of assessment approaches.

In Chapter 4 of this book it was emphasised that assessing capacity is a time-consuming process. The BPS guidance (2006), published prior to the implementation of the MCA, discusses the issue of service constraints and available time in relation to capacity assessments. It was envisaged that a capacity assessment would be part of routine clinical work for clinical psychologists, and suggested that a 20-minute interview may suffice for straightforward cases, but more complex ones may need several hours. Given the advisory role of an EP in capacity assessments, it is more likely that the young people referred will be more complex.

Walji *et al.* (2014) noted that clinical psychologists actually take 45–155 minutes to undertake a capacity assessment. This time frame reflects the author's own experience of undertaking capacity assessments with young adults with learning difficulties or disabilities on behalf of the official solicitor. The assessment was to ascertain if the young adult had the capacity to instruct a solicitor in relation to proceedings in the Family Court. Prior to the assessment, the author was supplied with the court file, so had some background information about the young adult, and the local authority's concerns about the young adult's ability to parent. In all cases, the young adult did not know the author so some time was spent building rapport. This enabled the author to become familiar with the young adult's communication style and ascertain their understanding of language. The shortest actual assessment was probably about 45 minutes with a woman who had severe learning difficulties; the longest about two hours with a young dyslexic father who was a frequent cannabis user.

## Conclusion

There are few publications or specific guidance for applied psychologists in relation to undertaking capacity assessments. The BPS (2006) guidance was written prior to the implementation of the MCA and focuses on clinical psychologists' practice. The 2010 BPS and SCIE audit tool provides for practical reflection on a capacity assessment enabling a psychologist to improve their practice. Although this is written for applied psychologists in healthcare settings, it is appropriate for EPs, and could be adapted to reflect EP practice. A recent study about clinical psychologists' experiences provides issues for EPs to consider. However, all these publications and the MCA COP indicate that the expected way of working is routine practice for EPs. The advisory nature of the EP role in a capacity assessment is similar to the consultative model practised by many EP services.

Walji *et al.* (2014) focused on the practicalities of implementing the MCA, and bemoaned the lack of appropriate resources, but did not suggest that clinical psychologists undertake research and evaluation activities to plug the gap. EPs sometimes undertake small-scale research projects. Since working with the 16–25 age range is a developing area, EPs may be motivated to undertake projects exploring approaches and resources to develop decision-making abilities in young people with SEN. Whilst young people would benefit from ways to promote general decision-making, education establishment staff, and local authority SEN officers probably need strategies and resources focusing on enabling young people to make educational decisions. Particularly tricky issues relate to helping young people understand the abstract concept of the local authority and its role in managing the EHC Plan. Perhaps these areas lend themselves to trainee EP research projects.

## Summary of issues to be considered

- Adoption of Atkinson *et al.*'s (2015) competency framework for EPs working with young people aged 16–25.

- Production of:
    - service guidance for EPs
    - information about the advisory role of an EP in relation to capacity assessments for young people, parents, local authority officers and educational establishment staff
    - service capacity assessment record forms.

- Ensuring the required amount of time can be allocated to a particular capacity assessment.

- Appropriate training in MCA principles and capacity assessments.

- MCA and capacity assessments as part of the induction of EPs and trainee EPs new to the service.

- Inclusion of MCA and capacity assessments as part of EP doctoral training.

- Use of the BPS and SCIE capacity assessment audit tool as part of continuing professional development.

- Consideration of opportunities to undertake research and development focusing on facilitating decision-making in young people with SEN.

# Part 3

# Education Professionals, the Young Person and Their Family

*Chapter 7*

# Resolving Disagreements about the Outcome of a Mental Capacity Assessment

Returning to the quotes at the beginning of Chapter 1 epitomises the struggle some parents may have in accepting that their young person with special educational needs (SEN), or mental health, issues can make their own decisions about some matters. This suggests there will be occasions when the view that a young person has capacity to make a decision may be challenged by parents, as the young person's choice takes precedence over what parents believe is best for their offspring. Equally, disagreements can arise if the young person is deemed not to have capacity to make the particular decision. The outcome of a capacity assessment may be disputed by another education, health or social care professional. In all cases, the dispute resolution process is the same.

Chapter 4 advocates that an assessor records the capacity assessment process formally on an appropriately constructed form (see Appendix 1). If the outcome of a capacity assessment is challenged, an assessor will need to show they have applied the MCA principles (MCA COP 4.64), conducted a fair assessment and have evidence to support their conclusion. A fully completed capacity assessment record form will greatly assist an assessor providing the required information.

## Resolving disputes about the outcome of a capacity assessment

The MCA COP (4.63–4.65) sets out a process to facilitate resolving differences of opinion, and the MCA COP Chapter 15 provides information about more formalised dispute resolution, but this is focused on health and social care systems. There is a section on mediation as a disagreement resolution process; all the services suggested charge fees. The SEND COP Chapter 11 explains how disagreements are resolved relating to a young person's SEN. A local authority has to provide a free impartial disagreement resolution service to help resolve differences of opinion between a young person with SEN, or their parent, and the educational establishment or local authority, irrespective of whether the young person has an Education, Health and Care (EHC) Plan. It is likely that this service may be able to support a young person, or their parent, raising their concerns about the outcome of a capacity assessment. Information about this service should be part of the Local Offer (see the Glossary). A local authority also has to offer a free mediation service, but this is restricted to decisions about EHC Plans that are going to be the subject of an appeal to the Special Educational Needs and Disability (SEND) Tribunal. Alternatively, parents or a young person may be supported by another organisation or voluntary body.

Educational establishments and local authorities already have complaints procedures and associated documentation; it is advisable to produce easy-to-understand information about the disagreement resolution process relating to the outcome of a capacity assessment, including organisations that can offer support to the young person, or parent, such as the local Impartial information, advice and support service. Below, the author proposes a staged disagreement resolution process following the MCA COP system but appropriate to education.

## Proposed disagreement resolution process for disputes about the outcome of capacity assessment
### Level 1: Low key approach

The MCA COP (15.3) advises that efforts should be made to resolve disagreements before they become serious disputes, highlighting the role of good communication, including listening to the concerns. This suggests that the assessor should arrange to meet with those who are challenging the outcome of the capacity assessment rather than communicating in writing. If the person disputing the outcome of the assessment is an education, health or social care professional, rather than a parent or young person, email or phone communication would be appropriate. However, protracted correspondence suggests a meeting may be advisable.

The assessor should:

- arrange a meeting as soon as possible with the young person or parent raising the concern, at a mutually convenient time for all concerned, so they can explain their reasons for and provide evidence to support their conclusion about the young person's capacity or lack of it (MCA COP 4.63–4) or

- contact the education, health or social care professional disputing the outcome of the capacity assessment by phone or email as soon as possible.

In both cases, the assessor needs to demonstrate how they have applied the MCA principles and conducted a fair assessment, including showing that:

- they communicated with the young person in their preferred way

- they could understand the young person's communication

- they gave the young person time to respond

- the young person was comfortable in the situation

- information was presented to the young person in their preferred format, for example, photos, videos, pictures, sign language, braille, moon easy-read text, etc.

- memory aids were used to help the young person

- the young person was able or unable to understand the information

- the young person was able or unable to make a choice using the information
- the young person did or did not communicate their choice
- they repeated the process again at a later date to confirm the young person could or could not make the decision.

If this meeting is unable to resolve the matter, the assessor should progress to Level 2.

## *Level 2: More formalised meeting*

The assessor should explain to whoever is disputing the outcome of the capacity assessment that the assessor could arrange:

- a second opinion – this may be from another member of the school or college staff, a specialist teacher or possibly an educational psychologist followed by either:

    a) a meeting with both assessors. The second assessor would also need to demonstrate how they have upheld the MCA principles and had undertaken a fair assessment, including the bullet point list in Level 1, or

    b) a meeting with both assessors, chaired by someone from the Impartial information, advice and support services or other organisation such as a voluntary body, to facilitate discussions.

If the young person or parent opts for (b), it is important they are given information about organisations that can support them during the meeting, such as the local authority's Impartial information, advice and support services.

If the issue is not resolved, then the assessor(s) should inform whoever is disputing the outcome of the capacity assessment about the options open to them. All the courses of action now involve more formalised processes and are likely to have fees attached, as well as taking time.

## Level 3: Formal processes

If there is continuing disagreement regarding the young person's capacity to make the particular decision, the matter may need to be resolved more formally. There are free legal helplines, such as the Coram Children's Legal Centre[1] and NYAS[2] that may be able to assist. The Education Law Association[3] lists solicitors firms that specialise in education law. Chambers and Partners[4] lists law firms specialising in Court of Protection work.

### Court of Protection

As noted in Chapter 2 of this book, the Court of Protection[5] hears cases where there is a dispute about a young person's capacity to make a particular decision. Whoever is disputing the outcome of the capacity assessment may consider making an application, but there are associated costs.

## Summary

- The outcome of a capacity assessment can be challenged by the young person, their parent or a professional.

- In the event of a challenge, the assessor will need to demonstrate how they upheld the MCA principles, conducted a fair assessment and have evidence to support their conclusion.

- The MCA COP (4.63–4.65 and Chapter 15) sets out dispute resolution processes, but these are focused on health and social care systems.

---

1   www.childrenslegalcentre.com.
2   www.nyas.net.
3   www.educationlawassociation.org.uk.
4   www.chambersandpartners.com.
5   www.gov.uk/court-of-protection.

- The MCA COP highlights the role of good communication in resolving disputes.
- A graduated three-stage dispute resolution process was proposed appropriate to education.

# Chapter 8

# 'Best Interests' and 'Best Interests' Checklist

The 'best interests' principle of the Mental Capacity Act (MCA) 2005 only applies when a capacity assessment has concluded that, on the balance of probabilities, the young person lacks capacity to make this decision about their education. In this circumstance, the Children and Families Act 2014 stipulates that it will be the young person's parent or representative who makes the decision on their behalf (Special Educational Needs and Disability Code of Practice (SEND COP) Annex 1). However, for decisions relating to the content of an Education, Health and Care (EHC) Plan, the parent may make choices about what they wish to be included, amended or removed, but the final decision rests with the local authority. This raises the issue of whether the local authority Special Educational Needs (SEN) officer should be following the 'best interests' checklist. Interestingly, the SEND COP Chapter 9 *Education Health and Care Needs Assessments and Plans* omits the MCA from the relevant legislation listed at the beginning of the chapter. Despite local authority SEN officers, like all those working in education with young people, being required to have regard to the MCA, the regulations relating to drawing up and managing EHC Plans have to take precedence. However, it would be good practice for local authority SEN officers to familiarise themselves with the 'best interests' checklist, and to use it as a guide whenever possible.

Whilst the local authority SEN officer is able to override parental wishes without regard to the 'best interests' checklist, in relation to the content of the EHC Plan, the young person, or their parent, can challenge the local authority's decisions made in relation to Sections B (SEN), F (special educational provision required) and I (name and type of educational establishment by appealing to the Special Educational Needs and Disability (SEND) Tribunal).

Thus, generally education professionals, unlike their health and social care colleagues, will very rarely make a 'best interests' decision on behalf of a young person who lacks capacity to do so. The most likely instance when an education professional will decide on behalf of a young person is in their role as corporate parent for a young person in public care.

Nevertheless, education professionals do need to know about the MCA 'best interests' checklist as a capacity assessment that concludes the young person lacks capacity means a young person's parent, or representative, will be making the decision using 'best interests' principles. During the course of a capacity assessment, the assessor should ensure they record both verbal and non-verbal behaviours that give an insight into the young person's views, wishes and feelings about the choices (see Chapter 4). This information can then be passed to the parent to use as part of their decision-making under the 'best interests' process. The 'best interests' checklist encourages parents to consult other people, for example, educational establishment staff, who may have information about the young person in relation to the decision, including their wishes, feelings, beliefs and values.

Like the outcome of a capacity assessment, a 'best interests' decision can be challenged. The 'best interests' process set out in the Mental Capacity Act 2005 Code of Practice (MCA COP) Chapter 5 assumes it will be a health or social care professional who makes the decision on behalf of the young person who lacks capacity to do so. So a dispute about a 'best interests' decision in health and social care would be initiated by the young person's parents to challenge a professional's choice. However, the way the MCA has been incorporated into the Children and Families Act 2014, for educational decisions, means that it is an education, health or social care professional who is disagreeing with the parents' 'best interests' decision and who will launch a challenge to the parents' choice. This is undoubtedly a very uncomfortable position for education professionals, which could, potentially, adversely affect their relationship with the young person's parents and possibly the young person as well. Nonetheless, education professionals have to have regard to the MCA COP and so have a responsibility to ensure decisions taken on behalf of a young person are in their 'best interests', and if appropriate, limit their rights and freedoms as little as possible (see Chapter 2 in this book). Therefore, if an education professional has a concern, they need to consider raising this with the young person's parent. The MCA 5.68 sets out a dispute resolution process, discussed below.

## 'Best interests'

'Best interests' does not have an actual definition either in the MCA itself, or in the MCA COP; it is guidance set out in the 'best interests' checklist' (see Appendix 3) that is summarised in the MCA COP Chapter 5. The person making the decision on behalf of a young person who lacks capacity to make the particular decision is known as the decision-maker. For educational decisions, the decision-maker will be the young person's parent or representative if they have one. To act in a young person's 'best interests' the decision-maker must ensure the decision is not what they would choose if presented with the options (MCA COP 5.7) or what they would want for the young person (MCA COP 4.49), but the choice the young person would have made if they were able to do so. The MCA COP Chapter 5 urges the decision-maker to do everything they reasonably can to work out what is in the young person's 'best interests'; this means following the 'best interests' checklist.

If a capacity assessment establishes that the young person lacks capacity to make the decision, the assessor will need to discuss with the young person's parents about making the decision in the young person's 'best interests'. The assessor should advise the parent to follow the 'best interests' checklist' in the MCA COP Chapter 5 to ensure they have, on balance, acted in their young person's best interest. As noted in Chapter 2, parents do have to follow the MCA but not the MCA COP, although they are encouraged to follow the MCA COP as this explains the expectations. This assumes that the young person's parents have the requisite literacy skills to read and understand the 'best interests' checklist, as well as keeping a record of how they made the decision. Mencap have produced a simplified 'best interests' checklist using the acronym 'Reflect' in their mental capacity resource pack publication for families (Mencap undated). As the booklet is focused on health decisions, one of the items was not relevant to educational decisions, so the author has adapted it and added visual prompts. This simplified checklist would be suitable to use with Tactile Talk Technology™ (PENpal produced by Mantra Lingua), which would increase its accessibility to parents who have limited access to written English. Alternatively, creating a CD ROM would enable the written and visual information to be supplemented with audio information that would provide the opportunity to offer further explanation and examples.

An internet search for video/audio materials to explain the MCA and 'best interests' found various videos produced by health and social care organisations, but these focused on particular populations such as the elderly. The Social Care Institute for Excellence (SCIE) has its own videos, but only one would seem be of interest to education professionals.[1] There were no videos that may be helpful to parents, and many would probably be confusing.

Several NHS trusts and social care departments have developed a 'best interests' balance sheet to facilitate making 'best interests' decisions. This is an approach advocated by SCIE for difficult or contentious decisions. The author has devised one to be given to parents, or used during a 'best interests' meeting if there is a concern about a decision made by parents (see Appendix 3). Some parents may be daunted by the responsibility of making a 'best interests' decision, such as choosing an educational establishment; education professionals could offer to work with the parent using the 'best interests' checklist and balance sheet to help make the decision.

---

1  'Khurrum's move', MCA making 'best interests' decisions; see www.scie.org.uk/socialcaretv.

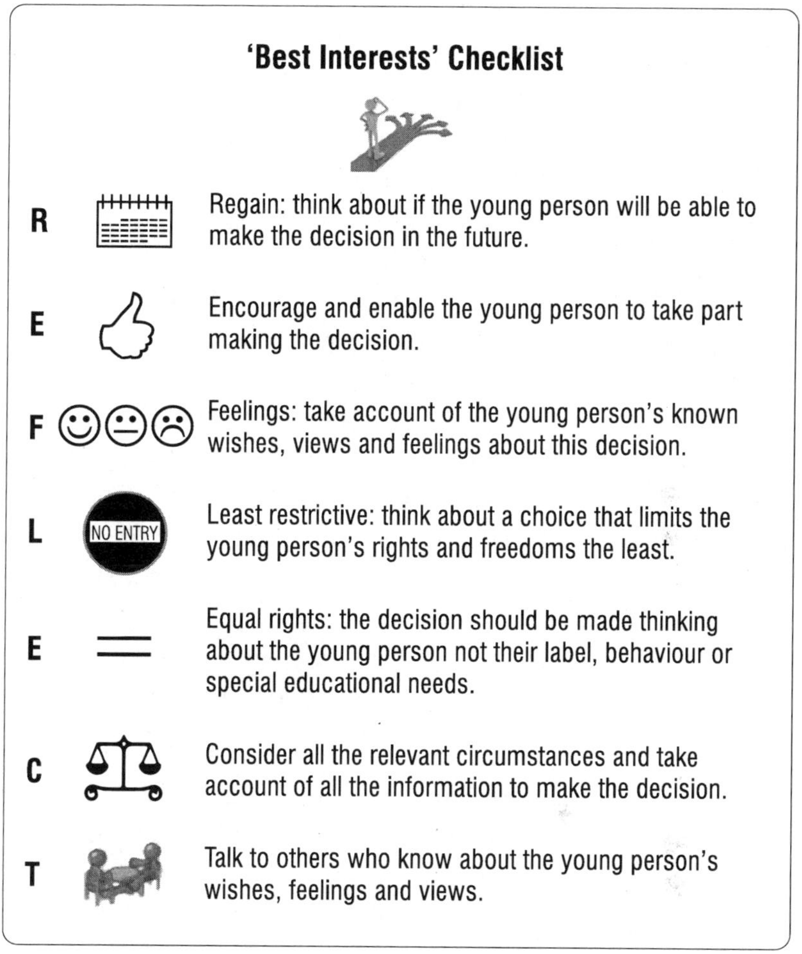

## 'Best Interests' Checklist

**R** — Regain: think about if the young person will be able to make the decision in the future.

**E** — Encourage and enable the young person to take part making the decision.

**F** — Feelings: take account of the young person's known wishes, views and feelings about this decision.

**L** — Least restrictive: think about a choice that limits the young person's rights and freedoms the least.

**E** — Equal rights: the decision should be made thinking about the young person not their label, behaviour or special educational needs.

**C** — Consider all the relevant circumstances and take account of all the information to make the decision.

**T** — Talk to others who know about the young person's wishes, feelings and views.

Figure 8.1 Simplified 'best interests' checklist, adapted from Mencap

## 'Best interests' checklist (MCA COP 5.13–5.28, 5.37–5.61)

Sometimes this checklist is referred to as the statutory 'best interests' checklist. It is described in the MCA COP (5.6) as a checklist of common factors that must always be considered by the decision-maker, although not all will be relevant to every decision. The MCA COP (5.7) emphasises the decision-maker should take into account all the relevant factors, and not just those they think are important. The 'best interests' checklist is considered the starting point for making a 'best interests' decision, and there may be other factors that should be taken into account for a particular decision. The MCA COP (5.14) indicates that a young person's 'best interests' may change over time and should be regularly reviewed. For a young person with an EHC Plan, educational decisions are reviewed on an annual basis; it could be good practice to use the 'best interests' checklist to assist with this process.

The full 'best interests' checklist includes healthcare matters that are not relevant to education; these have been omitted from the discussion below.

It is expected that the decision-maker will work through each item on the checklist; some may be more relevant than others to the particular decision. However, the first item on the list always applies, as does consideration of the young person's wishes, feelings and views. Ideally, the young person ought to be encouraged to participate in decision-making as far as they are able to do so. In the event of a 'best interests' decision being challenged, the decision-maker should be able to show how they followed the checklist.

- 'Best interests' decisions should not be based on the young person's condition, diagnosis, label, age or the way they look or behave. It should be based on carefully considering the 'best interests' checklist.

---

Jill has learning difficulties and is following a life skills course at the local further education (FE) college. For the next academic year she has to choose between personal care, which includes fashion, hair and beauty, and cooking options. She likes fashion, styling her younger sister's and her own hair, and is beginning to wear some make-up. She has no interest in making herself snacks or learning to cook a meal. A capacity assessment for this choice considered that, on the balance of probabilities, she lacked the capacity to make the decision, so her mother will choose. Jill's mother feels that the personal care option is less useful to Jill as someone with learning difficulties than learning to prepare snacks. Therefore, she picks the cooking option.

In this scenario, Jill's mother has considered Jill's learning difficulties as the main reason for the decision rather than what Jill herself may have chosen. Therefore, in this case, Jill's mother was not acting in Jill's 'best interests', but what she thought was best for her.

- It should be considered whether the young person may, at a later date, be able to make the particular decision – for example, if the young person is experiencing a serious deterioration in their mental health, which may improve with treatment, or if they are receiving specific support to develop their communication skills, or learning something relevant to making this decision. Some choices are needed by a specific date; this time frame may preclude the young person from being able to make the particular decision, so their parent will have to choose.

- Every effort should be made to encourage the young person to participate in making the decision. This accords with the SEND COP principle of young people participating as fully as possible in making decisions. The MCA COP also notes that young people should be assisted to improve their decision-making ability. As noted in Chapter 3 in this book, decision-making could be considered as an outcome in an EHC Plan or person-centred plan.

- It is important to identify all the factors the young person themselves would take into account if they were making this decision. These issues may be part of the 'best interests' checklist or additional ones. However, the decision-maker would only be expected to consider matters they are aware of and it would be reasonable to regard as relevant.

> Jill likes looking after animals; she has a cat and a rabbit at home. She does not like to see animals being hurt and becomes upset if she sees animals on television being killed or having an operation. Jill has to choose between animal care or horticulture options with associated work experience. She would probably choose the animal care option, but would ask not to see animals being hurt. Following a capacity assessment Jill has, on the balance of probabilities, been considered to lack capacity to make her own choice, therefore her parents will decide.

Given what is known about Jill, it could be assumed that her parents would pick the animal care option, as this is more likely to have been Jill's own choice. Choosing animal care takes account of Jill's interest and experience. It would also be expected that Jill's parents would make known her dislike of seeing animals hurt, which has implications for potential work experience placements. Ideally, her parents ought to clearly state that Jill's work experience should not expose her to seeing animals being, in her view, hurt. Depending on the type of accommodation Jill lives in and the interests of her family, she may have no experience of seeing someone garden or grow indoor plants. Thus, it would probably be most unexpected for the horticulture option to be chosen on her behalf.

- The decision-maker must consider in particular the young person's views, wishes and feelings. These may have been ascertained in a variety of ways:
  - the young person may have, recently or in the past, made their views, wishes and feelings known about the choices. This may have been communicated verbally or by their behaviour to their parents and/or educational establishment staff. For example, a young person has been in a similar situation in the past and behaved

in a particular way that helps understand the choice they would make; or the young person's views, wishes and feelings may have been demonstrated during the capacity assessment. Whoever undertook the capacity assessment should have recorded these on the capacity assessment form and passed this information to the decision-maker

- o the young person may have beliefs and values (for example, religious, cultural, moral or political) that they would consider when making the particular decision.

---

Jill does not like to see animals hurt; even an animal having an operation upsets her. However, Jill's love of animals means the animal care option would be her choice, if she had been deemed to have capacity to choose. Jill's dislike of seeing animals hurt would mean that a work experience placement at a vet's surgery would be inappropriate. Therefore, the decision-maker (Jill's parents) ought to explain to the FE college that Jill's animal care work experience should be somewhere she will not see animals undergoing surgical procedures, such as a kennels or animal sanctuary.

---

- The decision-maker is encouraged to consult other people to take account of their views about what would be in the 'best interests' of the young person who lacks capacity to make the decision. This book focuses on decisions about the young person's education, so it may be appropriate, depending on the decision, for the young person's parents, as decision-maker, to consult with the young person's:

    - o educational establishment staff or specialist teachers
    - o speech and language therapist, physiotherapist, occupational therapist or educational psychologist

- o mental health professional
- o social worker.
- The options that are the least restrictive of the young person's rights should be considered. This is illustrated in the scenario below.

> The college is organising a number of fund-raising events on Children in Need day. Jill's life skills course is baking cakes to sell on two cake stalls, one in college, the second at a local social services day centre. Jill is very keen to sell the cakes as well as bake them. She is considered, on the balance of probabilities, to lack capacity to decide which cake stall she would like to sell the cakes; her mother is asked to choose. The group going to the day centre will be walking there and back. Jill would need 1:1 support on the walk and to be with her selling the cakes, as her speech is very unclear; she can become very frustrated when she cannot be understood. She does use Makaton, but this would not be understood by the day centre service users or staff. The college cake stall will be in the canteen. Jill is well known in the college and many students and staff know a few Makaton signs. If Jill sold cakes at the college-based cake stall, she would not need 1:1 support, just the supervision planned for the cake stall. Jill's mother chooses the college cake stall as this is the least restrictive option.

- When the decision-maker has worked through the checklist and gathered the information, they will need to weigh up all the factors to work out which option is in their young person's 'best interests'.

## What 'best interests' decisions will parents make in relation to education?

Educational decisions can be broadly categorised as relating to the following.

### *The content of an EHC Plan*

As noted above, parents may decide the content they wish to have included, amended or removed from the EHC Plan, but the final decision rests with the local authority. These wishes are usually communicated during an annual review meeting, and recorded in the annual review paperwork, for consideration by the local authority. Thus, if educational establishment, health or social care professionals present at the meeting are concerned the proposed decision is not in the young person's 'best interests', they should tactfully explain their concerns to the parents. This difference of opinion must be recorded in the annual review paperwork, so the local authority is made aware of the concerns, and these can be considered when the local authority makes the decision. This means that there is nothing further that an education, health or social care professional needs do in relation to their misgivings.

### *Curricular choices within the educational establishment*

Some choices within the education establishments, for example, options and work experience, when picked, are written into the EHC Plan. However, it is the educational establishment that offers the option and work experience placements, not the local authority. In this case, educational establishment staff ought to consider whether the choice, made by a parent on behalf of their young person who lacks capacity, is in the young person's 'best interests'. If there are concerns that the parents' choices are not in the young person's 'best interests', educational establishment staff should follow the dispute resolution process described below.

## Extracurricular and social activities within and organised by the educational establishment

As noted in previous chapters, educational establishments offer a wider range of activities than just the taught curriculum. Several case studies have highlighted choices relating to extracurricular or social events. Occasionally participation in these may become an EHC Plan outcome or provision, although generally the young person's participation is not part of their special educational provision. Like curricular and EHC Plan choices, if the young person is considered, on the balance of probabilities, to lack capacity to decide, this is done on their behalf. 'Best interests' applies to these choices. In Chapter 2, it was established that the young person's parents or representative would most likely decide on the young person's behalf.

Returning to the scenario above of Jill selling cakes, if her parent had chosen for Jill to sell the cakes at the day centre, college staff may have been concerned that this was not in Jill's 'best interests'. In this event, college staff ought to, tactfully, raise their misgivings with Jill's parent. Some education professionals may feel that, whilst Jill's parent's choice would not have been theirs as it means Jill is continuously supervised, it is a very short-term activity and as such, it may not be helpful to raise concerns that may damage the relationship with Jill's mother. This may be a pragmatic response to this decision; nevertheless, education professionals have to consider the implications of ignoring their concerns about parental decisions that may not be in the young person's 'best interests'. Realistically, perhaps being selective about which parental decisions are questioned may successfully achieve the goal of helping parents shift their thinking from what they want to what it is their young person would have chosen. Disputing every parental choice educational professionals believe is not in the young person's 'best interests' may only serve to alienate parents, which ultimately is not in the young person's best interests.

## What if an education professional considers the parents' decision is not in the young person's 'best interests'?

The first parental quote at the start of Chapter 1 epitomises the beliefs of countless parents that they know what their young person wants. For the education professional, heeding the words, 'Be kind, for everyone you meet is fighting a hard battle' (Anon, sometimes attributed to Plato), is wise counsel to consider when expressing concerns that the parents' decision may not be in the young person's 'best interests'. Hopefully, this will be a very rare event, but should it occur, the situation needs to be managed with great sensitivity.

As noted above, the dispute resolution process set out in the MCA COP (5.68) assumes that a health or social care professional is the decision-maker if the young person lacks capacity. Nevertheless, for educational decisions the Children and Families Act 2014 states it is the young person's parent or representative. Consequently, in the absence of an appropriate formalised disagreement resolution system, the author proposes one for educational establishment choices, such as options, work experience placements, participation in extracurricular activities or social events, based on the MCA COP process and the BPS guidance (2007) for a 'best interests' meeting. Some NHS trusts and social services departments have adopted the latter.

However, any disagreement resolution process is predicated on the process used to arrive at the disputed decision. The MCA COP Chapter 5 sets out a 'best interests' procedure, advising health and social care professionals to keep records of their decision-making process (5.15), in particular noting:

- how the decision was reached
- the reasons for the decision
- who was consulted to assist working out the young person's 'best interests'
- the particular factors taken into account.

However, for educational decisions, it is the parents, not an education professional, who will choose on behalf of a young person who lacks capacity. It is unrealistic to expect a parent to keep a written record of their decision-making process. This has a direct impact on the dispute resolution process because it is based on the decision-maker being able to show how they have worked through the 'best interests' checklist, and arrived at their choice.

From the options set out in the MCA COP (5.68), the only viable one for the parent as the decision-maker is for the educational professional concerned to convene what is referred to as a formal or informal 'best interests' case conference. The BPS (2007) document describes a very formal meeting format, which seems to have been quite widely adopted. It advocates that the meeting is chaired by someone experienced in managing meetings, but who is independent of the decision being made. Attendees should be those who hold relevant information, including the wishes and feelings of the young person, and knowledge of the pros and cons of the options under discussion. The aim is to work through the 'best interests' checklist to arrive at a consensus that, on the balance of probabilities, selects the option that is in the young person's 'best interests'.

However, within education it is an education professional challenging parents' choice; this needs the utmost tact and diplomacy. Sir Isaac Newton described tact as the art of making a point without making an enemy. This seems very relevant to the situation, as it is important to endeavour to preserve relationships whilst expressing concerns. The BPS guidance (2007) describes a meeting akin to an annual review, although this would appear to be a somewhat confrontational approach for education professionals to assume.

As previously noted, the MCA COP places emphasis on good communication as a means of resolving differences of opinion. Hence, perhaps the starting point is for just the education professional(s) concerned about the decision to meet with the young person's parents to talk about their misgivings, using the 'best interests' checklist to structure the discussion, and a balance sheet to record it. Nevertheless, the meeting should not begin to resemble an annual review meeting; limiting the number of education professionals to two may be advisable, and ideally this should include the assessor. If another professional, for example, an educational psychologist (EP), assisted the assessor, it may be appropriate to invite them to this meeting. Communicating with the parent by email or by text to express the concerns is likely to lead to misunderstandings and misinterpretation. On the other hand, parents have busy lives, and attending an unexpected meeting may be very difficult. It is the face-to-face nature of this meeting that is important to discuss such a sensitive issue. An acceptable compromise would be a Skype/VOIP conversation at a mutually convenient time. It would be good practice to inform the parent they can seek support from the Impartial information, advice and support service for this meeting.

In the meeting, whether in person or via Skype/VOIP, the education professional(s) should use the 'best interests' checklist to facilitate the discussion, with the aim of understanding the process the parents used to make their decision, including all the factors considered, anyone consulted and the reasons for the choice. Additionally, the education professional(s) should have the capacity assessment record form, so that they are aware of any views, wishes and feelings the young person expressed or demonstrated about the decision during the capacity assessment. By the end of the meeting, the education professionals ought to know how the parents arrived at their decision and whether, on balance, it is in the young person's 'best interests'. The education professional(s) should clearly state at the end of the meeting whether they now agree, that on balance, the decision is in the young person's 'best interests'. If the education professional(s) continue to have concerns, they must tell the parents about these, and what they will do next, if anything, although the options are limited (see below).

Following the meeting, the education professional(s) should send/email the parents a copy of the meeting minutes, including the balance sheet, within two days of the meeting. The minutes should clearly note whether the education professional now agrees that the parents' decision is in the young person's 'best interests'. If there is continuing disagreement, the education professional should record this in the minutes and their intended next steps. A copy should be placed on the young person's file. Like a capacity assessment record, this information is not for general distribution, but should be shared with those who are involved with the decision. If there are safeguarding concerns, the information may need to be given to the educational establishment safeguarding team, and possibly passed to the relevant social care professionals.

Some parental decisions will be presented as part of the annual review meeting, but it is the local authority's decision whether or not these are incorporated into the EHC Plan. Nonetheless, those at the meeting should make it known to the parents if they have concerns about the choices being in the young person's 'best interests', and any differences of opinion recorded in the annual review paperwork.

So what happens if the educational professionals still consider that, on balance, the parents' decision is not in the young person's 'best interests'? Hopefully, this will be an extremely rare occurrence. It is difficult to suggest a graduated course of action; the processes advised in the MCA COP are not applicable to the parent as decision-maker, except for recourse to the Court of Protection. The possible options depend on the nature of the decision or the concern.

The options for a parental decision causing concern are as follows.

- If it is the subject of an appeal to the First-tier SEND Tribunal (the Tribunal), the education professional should make the local authority SEN officer managing the young person's EHC Plan aware of their misgivings and provide a record of the meeting with the parents.

- If it raises safeguarding issues, the education professional would be advised to follow the educational establishment's safeguarding procedures.

- If it relates to a within college choice, such as options or participation in an activity, where the decision seems not to have taken account of the all the relevant information, such as the known wishes, feelings and views of the young person, the education professional could:

- seek a second opinion from a colleague, using the 'best interests' checklist and balance sheet completed in the meeting with the parent and/or
- discuss the continuing concerns with their line manager or senior member of staff.

• As a last resort, the education professional could make an application to the Court of Protection, although this will incur costs and take time.

## Summary of the proposed process for resolving disagreements with parents

- The education professional(s) concerned about the parental decision can convene a meeting with the parent, either in person or via Skype/VOIP. To avoid overwhelming the parent, it may be advisable to limit the number of educational professionals to two.
- At the meeting, the education professionals:
  - use the 'best interests' checklist to structure the discussion and record it on a 'best interests' balance sheet
  - state at the end if they now, on balance, agree that the decision is in the young person's 'best interests'
  - if they continue to have concerns, inform the parent what they will do next
  - record their stance in the meeting minutes.
- After the meeting, the education professionals will send/email the parent the meeting minutes and 'best interests' balance sheet, and place copies in the young person's file.

## Summary

- 'Best interests' does not have an actual definition, either in the MCA or the MCA COP; it is guidance set out in the 'best interests' checklist.

- The MCA COP assumes that it is the health or social care professional making the 'best interests' decision on behalf of the young person.

- The person making the 'best interests' decision is referred to as the decision-maker.

- For educational decisions it is the parent or young person's representative who is the decision-maker.

- Parents have to follow the MCA 'best interests' checklist when making a decision on behalf of their young person.

- If an educational professional is concerned that a parental decision is not in the young person's 'best interests', they should meet face-to-face with the parents to discuss the matter.

- The education professional should use the 'best interests' checklist to structure the discussion. The author proposes a disagreement resolution process if an educational professional is concerned a parent's decision is not in the young person's 'best interests'.

# Chapter 9

# Supporting and Working with Parents

Thus far, the book has addressed circumstances when there is a difference of opinion between the education professional and a young person's parents – parents challenging education professionals when they do not agree with the outcome of a capacity assessment, or education professionals being concerned about a 'best interests' decision made by parents. However, the Children and Families Act 2014 places emphasis on education professionals working with young people and their parents to enable young people to succeed and make a successful transition to adulthood. Education professionals must have regard to the wishes and feelings of the young person and their parents, with the focus changing to the young person on their 16th birthday. In relation to the Mental Capacity Act (MCA) 2005, education professionals are likely to find themselves either supporting a parent whose young person has capacity to make the decision, or working with parents who are making the decision on the young person's behalf because they lack capacity to do so. This chapter presents suggestions to foster positive relationships with parents to promote a young person's independence.

The parental quotes in Chapter 1 are probably representative of parents' understanding of the transition, from them making decisions, to their young person making their own choices in education. These views are similar to those reported by Mitchell (2012), discussed below. For young people receiving support for their special educational needs (SEN) through the Special Educational Needs and Disability Code of Practice (SEND COP), the change is unequivocally set out in the SEND COP Chapter 8. In this chapter, the focus switches to the young person as the subject of the guidance rather than the parent. Parents and other family members can continue to support young people in making decisions, or act on their behalf, provided the young person is happy for them to do so (8.15): 'A young person can ask a family member or friend to support them in any way they wish' (8.18). Local authorities, schools and colleges are encouraged to involve parents in discussions about their young person's education and future plans (8.17). The SEND COP anticipates that a young person will usually discuss decisions about the content of their Education, Health and Care (EHC) Plan with their family, but emphasises that the final decision is the young person's (8.17).

Over the years, a young person's parents will have become experts in understanding their child's needs to advise others about these. Parental and family life is likely to have been adapted to support the young person. Parents are likely to have concerns about the shift from them as decision-makers to their young person making decisions. They may be worried that education professionals will over-estimate their young person's decision-making abilities, without understanding that their young person's level of functioning is related to the amount of support the parents are giving. Parents are likely to be anxious about feeling forced to withdraw support, as this may lead to the young person no longer being able to cope. Adjusting to the new expectations is likely to present challenges, and parents will need support to adapt to their changed role and accept that their young person should now be given every help and support to make their own decisions about their education and future.

Mitchell (2012) notes that there is a dearth of research exploring the process of decision-making within families with a young person with learning disabilities. Her study explores the factors parents consider when involving their young person (aged 13–21) with learning disabilities making a choice in the areas of education, health and care. Although Mitchell acknowledges the limitations of her small-scale study, it does give some insight into how parents facilitate, or hinder, their young person's participation in decision-making. She found that the parents' perception of a young person's ability to understand the relevant information influenced how far the parent enabled the young person to make the decision, or participate in the process; this was independent of the young person's age. However, it was not always the most important factor, or even considered. Other considerations related to the parents' views about the nature of the decision, for example, the significance or complexity, the desire to protect the young person, personal beliefs and attitudes and confidence in the practitioners. The relevant key findings from this study are that:

- Parents supported decision-making by simplifying the choices and, where possible, providing direct experience of the choice options. Parents presented the options based on their beliefs that they knew what was appropriate or best for their young person.

- The ability to actually experience the choices increased the young person's level of participation in the decision-making. It was noted specifically that, in education, where the young person was able to experience the options, for example, choosing a college, this appeared to support the young person's involvement in decision-making.

- The lower the possible risks involved with the decision, the more likely a young person would participate in making the choice.

- Parents did think they would have a reduced role in decision-making as the young person transitioned to adulthood. There was a shift in the parents' role to one of advocacy for their young person. This was particularly noted when the young person moved to a residential college or supported living accommodation. Parents acknowledged that there were now keyworkers/care staff who had a good knowledge of their young person and whose views should be considered in relation to decisions.

- Parents play an important role as information providers to both the young person and practitioners to support the young person when making significant life choices.

- Parents were concerned about their young person's needs and wishes being understood and valued, particularly if they had impaired communication.

- Practitioners need approaches and strategies for working with parents whom they believe are finding it difficult to allow their young person appropriate participation in decision-making. It is suggested that this may be a training need for practitioners.

The implications for education professionals relate to the development of their own knowledge and skills with regard to the Mental Capacity Act Code of Practice (MCA COP), including strategies and approaches to facilitate young people making choices, so they can confidently support parents to involve their young person as far as possible in all decision-making. It is essential that education professionals develop their understanding of the MCA, in the form of the MCA COP, to explain it to parents, highlighting parents' responsibilities in relation to it, as well as how it fits with the SEND COP. There are publications written for parents to support this (see, for example, Down's Syndrome Association 2014; Preparing for Adulthood 2015; Sinson 2015), but these are dependent on parents having the requisite reading skills. For those parents who have a good understanding of spoken language, but who find written materials more challenging, these publications could become accessible with free screen-reading software, for example, NVDA or Thunder. In 2006, the Department of Health published an easy-read guide to the Mental Capacity Act, but this is now out of date as it mainly refers to it starting later that year. As highlighted in Chapter 8, there appear to be no suitable audio or video resources to assist parents to comprehend the MCA and their responsibilities. The Council for Disabled Children (2014) has produced some short videos for young people that explain that, from their 16th birthday they can make their own choices; parents could be directed to these as a very brief introduction, although there is no actual reference to the MCA.

## Working positively and effectively with parents

Before education professionals can effectively support parents, they must be well prepared and secure in their knowledge, including knowing about capacity assessments and, if appropriate, how to undertake one (Chapter 4). Equally important is having clear policies and procedures, setting out how the MCA COP is implemented by education professionals within the educational establishment or local authority. This includes the process for expressing disagreements about the outcome of a capacity assessment, and how educational professionals will voice concerns to parents about a 'best interests' decision made on behalf of a young person who lacks capacity.

As part of safeguarding, it is important that there is an awareness of deprivation of liberty, and that this applies to foster homes, supported living arrangements, residential special schools and residential specialist colleges.

Just as necessary as the above are the education professionals' interpersonal skills, perceptions of their own competence in the area and their ability to build trust with the parent. As highlighted in Chapter 4, training in the MCA COP is essential, but equally important is training and guidance in working with parents. The ability to listen, communicate, show respect and having the requisite knowledge are key ingredients to working successfully with parents. This process could be initiated by working with the parent and young person to complete a Transitions Pathways Preparation for Adulthood style booklet.[1] This could lay the foundation for alerting the young person, and their parent, to some educational and life decisions the young person may need to make in the future, thereby affording the parent the opportunity to help prepare the young person for these choices.

---

1   See www.ndti.org.uk.

Easing parents' transition from being the decision-maker to enabling their young person to make their own choices may be facilitated by encouraging the young person, and their parent, to establish a Circle of Support (Foundation for People with Learning Disabilities 2015). This group supports the young person to achieve their educational and life goals, and means the young person has other people who know about their wishes and views.

## What education professionals need to know to be able to explain to parents

This section draws together information presented in depth in the preceding chapters, which will be noted in brackets, as well as suggesting practical strategies and approaches.

### Concepts and terms associated with the Mental Capacity Act

Those using a particular legislation tend to adopt the associated language. Parents will have become accustomed to the SEND COP language, but when their young person becomes 16, they will be introduced to new terminology, concepts and acronyms from the MCA COP. It is important that these are explained to parents in a way that is easily understood, including highlighting the differences between the language used in the MCA COP and SEND COP.

#### AGES

- 'Young person' in the SEND COP means someone aged 16–25, but in the MCA COP this term refers to someone aged 16–17 years 11 months. From 18 years old a young person is an adult.

- The SEND COP divides the age range as:
    - 0–16 years (end of compulsory schooling)
    - 16–18 years
    - 19–25 years.

- The MCA and MCA COP applies from a young person's 16th birthday (see Chapters 1 and 2); from then the young people should be making their own decisions. This is supported by the SEND COP, although it varies this age for decisions related to an EHC Plan.

- For decisions relating to the content of an EHC Plan, the young person can make these in their own right from the last Friday in June of their Year 11 (Y11) (see Chapter 1), rather than their parents doing so.

## Mental Capacity Act 2005

- Mental capacity means the ability to make a decision – any decision.

- The MCA five principles are set out in the MCA COP (see Chapter 2).

- It should be assumed that everyone can make their own decisions.

- A young person should have every support possible to enable them to make their own decision (MCA Principle 2).

- A young person should be involved at every step of making a particular choice, regardless of whether they will ultimately be able to make the decision when it is needed. Anything a young person says or shows through their behaviour is likely to give some insight into their views about the options.

- There is no such thing as general capacity; it is capacity per decision (see Chapters 2 and 3).

- A judgement about a young person's capacity cannot be based on a young person's diagnosis, label, condition, behaviour or appearance. Equally, being the subject of an EHC Plan has no bearing on a young person's capacity (see Chapters 3 and 4).

- Both the SEND and MCA COP place emphasis on the young person's views, wishes and feelings being taken into account.
- If there is a concern about a young person's ability to make a decision, they will be assessed to ascertain their capacity to make this particular decision (see Chapter 4).
- To be considered to possibly lack capacity, the young person must meet the capacity assessment Stage 1 criteria.
- Capacity is assessed using the 'four key questions'. Being unable to meet the requirements of one or more of the 'four key questions' means the young person lacks the capacity to make this decision at this time (see Chapter 4).
- The person undertaking a capacity assessment is known as the assessor.
- Parents should follow the MCA 'best interests' checklist when making a 'best interests' decision on behalf of their young person, who lacks capacity to make the particular decision. However, parents are advised to follow the MCA COP, as this is easier to understand than the actual law (see Chapter 8).
- A parent making a choice on behalf of a young person who lacks capacity is referred to as the decision-maker.
- Any choices parents make on behalf of the young person should be, as far as possible, the least restrictive options.

### Decisions

- The MCA COP categorises decisions into three types:
  - everyday decisions such as what to wear, what to eat etc.
  - 'more serious and significant' decisions: these have long-term effects and/or risks

- - ○ 'legal consequences' decisions such as personal budgets or appealing to the SEND Tribunal.
  - Decision-making is a part of developing independence; ideally decision-making should be an EHC Plan outcome.
  - Education professionals can show the parent how to support their young person making their own decisions (see below).

## How to convey the information to parents

There is a lack of suitable education-focused resources or information, presented in audio or video form (noted above and in other chapters). Nevertheless, education professionals will have to find a way of communicating the information to all parents of young people aged 16 and over, to ensure they are enabled to make their own decisions as far as possible. Given the range of parental literacy and language abilities, education professionals may have to be innovative; utilising the available ICT may assist creative solutions. CD ROMs, memory sticks and Tactile Talk Technology™ PENpal produced by Mantra Lingua could all assist in making written materials or information more accessible to parents. Developing a repertoire of verbal explanations and examples can be helpful, for example, to explain MCA principles, and parents' responsibility to make a decision in the young person's 'best interests'. The out-of-date Department of Health publication (2006), referred to above, included a simplified version of the MCA principles, which the author has adapted with visual prompts.

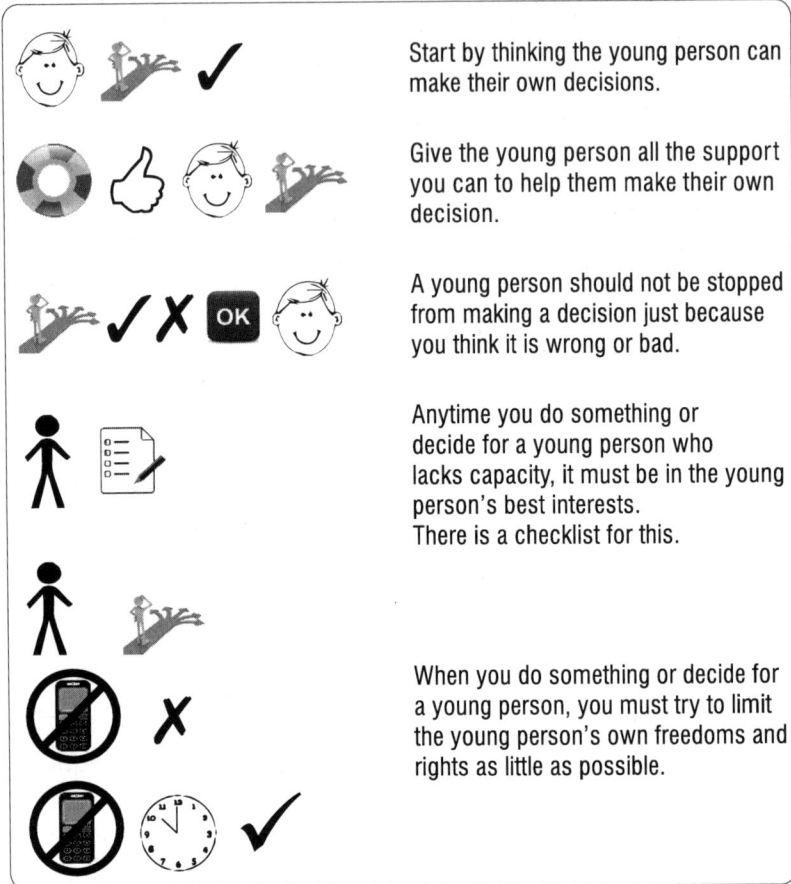

**Figure 9.1** Simplified version of the five principles of the Mental Capacity Act 2005 (adapted from Department of Health 2006)

### Making decisions

Even when a young person is considered to lack capacity to make a particular decision, there is an emphasis on a young person's wishes, views and feelings being taken into account. A young person's preferences will only be made known if they have been involved in the decision-making process. It is important that parents are encouraged to let their young person make whichever decisions, especially everyday choices, they are able to do, and to ensure they are part of all decision-making.

## Everyday Decisions

The Supreme Court ruling in March 2014 highlighted the importance of young people making everyday decisions. Developmentally these are the first choices that a young child is encouraged to make, and are very important for giving the young person some control of their life in terms of what they eat, wear or do. Some parents may feel that their young person's significant special needs mean that it is unlikely they can make choices. Education professionals will need to work with parents to facilitate young people being able to make these very basic choices at home. Emphasis should be placed on parents letting the young person experience the options as far as practicable. For example, if the young person is choosing food, they should be able to see, smell and taste the choices. As already noted, decision-making should ideally be written as an outcome in an EHC Plan. For example, Jill will be able to choose whether she would like juice or water to drink, or Jill will be able to choose whether she would like pizza or pasta for lunch, or Jill will be able to choose which lunch break activity she wishes to do.

At home, this could be extended to what clothes the young person wears, or food they eat for particular meals, or watches on television.

Mitchell (2012) found that parents facilitated their young person making choices by limiting the options presented to those the parents thought were the best or most appropriate. This is also noted by a parent in the National Autistic Society (2007) publication *Moving On Up*, who emphasised that her autistic daughter finds being presented with too many options stressful, so she needs to be given limited choices. In some ways, this goes against the spirit of the MCA, which places emphasis on a young person being made aware of all the options. For example, young people deciding what to wear should be doing so from what they have in their wardrobe – but for some young people it may be overwhelming to choose from the whole of their wardrobe; additionally, they may find it challenging to also consider the weather and temperature to choose appropriately. Yet if a parent or carer reduced the choices to two or three items for each layer of clothing that were suitable for the weather and activities, this could enable the young person to choose what they wear. Thus, for example, the young person may be able to choose between a cardigan and jumper and/or between a shirt and t-shirt. Given that the Supreme Court judges were concerned because the young people were not given any everyday choices, limiting the options would seem to be a pragmatic way of enabling young people to make some choices. However, it does raise some concerns, as the parent or carer is placing a restriction on what choices the young person is allowed to make as they control the options. This does not allow for young people experimenting or being rebellious in their choices, as their siblings who do not have disabilities may have done. Encouraging parents to allow their young person choices at the point of purchasing the clothes may go some way to address this inequality.

The Supreme Court judgment is, in effect, a commentary on the application of the MCA to date by publicly funded carers. The concerns raised by the judges seem to suggest that taking the MCA literally, in terms of having to offer a young person the full range of choices, in fact restricted the young person's opportunities to make choices rather than facilitating it. Therefore, some limiting of options offered to a young person may enable them to make a decision when this would not have been possible with the full range of choices. Nevertheless, parents ought to be encouraged to offer as many choices as possible to their young person.

To facilitate parents involving their young person in decision-making, the education professionals may wish to:

- produce a step-by-step guide for parents, which can be put on the educational establishment's or local authority's website, or printed off and given to parents. The advice could include:
    - a range of approaches, such as the use of visual materials, objects of reference and in particular, the young person actually experiencing the choices by smelling, touching, tasting, hearing and seeing

- giving practical examples of how to help a young person make particular choices, for example, clothing, what to eat
- use of ICT and appropriate software or apps
- explaining that the young person communicating their response may be through behavioural responses such as increased vocalisation or eye pointing
- explaining how things are referred to by the staff working with the young person, that is, vocabulary, signs, symbols, objects of reference
- information about helping the young person to set up a Circle of Support

- produce a DVD to lend to parents or podcast on the establishment's website
- advise parents of suitable apps, or readily available software, or ICT to support making choices
- hold a parents' workshop about helping young people to make decisions, including modelling how staff work with young people to facilitate decision-making
- set up a parents' group so parents can support each other
- encourage parents to allow their young person to establish a Circle of Support.

## 'More serious or significant' decisions

Regardless of whether parents believe the young person can, or cannot, make the decision, they should be encouraged to involve their young person at every step. If the young person is unable to make the particular decision, then their parent will do so on their behalf. Therefore, any discussion about enabling a young person to make a 'more serious or significant' decision will need to involve preparing the parent for the possibility they will be making the decision, if their young person lacks capacity to do so. This will entail

182 making parents aware of the MCA COP 'best interests' checklist and the importance of keeping a record of the young person's responses to the options, as these may indicate the young person's views, wishes and feelings about the choices. These will need to be taken into account by the parent if they are making the choice on behalf of their young person.

Suggested strategies and approaches to support parents include those suggested above, as well as:

- the use of objects of reference for each of the choices

- the importance of taking photos, videos and/or audio recordings of their young person experiencing the choices, so they can be used to remind the young person and their parents. Parents may need guidance about what to record

- giving practical examples of how to support a young person make the choice, for example, choosing a new educational establishment (see below)

- talking with young people about the options using all the support materials

- using visual images of smiley or sad faces or thumbs up, thumbs down for the young person to indicate their view of a particular choice, or aspect of the options under consideration

- ensuring parents and education professionals use the same vocabulary, signs, objects of reference or symbols, when talking with the young person about the choices. Education professionals will need to ask parents how they are referring to the choices.

If a new educational establishment is being proposed:

- The young person *must* visit *all* the places under consideration.

- Parents and education professionals should ensure they are using the same vocabulary, signs, objects of reference or symbols for the different places.

- During the visit, if possible, the young person should be taken to the areas that are of particular relevance to them, such as classrooms, specialist areas, as well as where they will eat their lunch, toileting facilities and to see break time activities.

- Visual and/or audio records of these visits should be used as a reminder. Photos or videos should include key areas in the educational establishment, such as classrooms, toileting facilities, dining areas and any specialist facilities to be used by the young person.

- The young person's responses, verbal and non-verbal/behavioural should be noted, as these may indicate the young person's views, wishes and feelings about the choices.

- Parents need to be encouraged to use these materials to talk with their young person about the choices. This may need to be modelled.

## 'Best interests'

All the suggested strategies and approaches above apply to supporting parents making a 'best interests' decision when the young person has been assessed as lacking capacity to make this decision. In this circumstance, it is important that parents are made aware of the 'best interests' checklist either as it appears in the MCA COP or a simplified version (see Chapter 8 in this book). Some parents may find a 'best interests' balance sheet helpful (see Appendix 3).

## Conclusion

The key to working effectively and positively with parents is communication, which is reinforced through both the SEND COP and MCA COP. It is essential that parents, young people and education professionals are using the same language to discuss the issues. Education professionals have an important part to play in supporting parents as they transition from being the decision-maker to supporting and enabling their young person to make choices about their education. Encouraging parents to become advocates for their young person could be a positive reframing of what some parents may perceive as a loss of their role, as their young person's autonomy is fostered. Overall, helping parents to enable their young person to make choices, especially everyday decisions, will probably give young people more opportunities to control what happens to them in keeping with the spirit of the MCA.

Some education professionals may feel this is quite onerous, but it should be seen as part of their own responsibilities to support young people making their own decisions. This is an integral part of developing a young person's independence, which is usually one of the desired outcomes of post-16 education. Just as working in partnership with parents is a long-established practice in the area of SEN, much of what is being suggested here is already the way in which education professionals work with young people with SEN. It is extending this to incorporate the MCA principles into everyday practice, explaining these to parents, as well as supporting them to allow their young person to make their own choices, and to take part in decision-making, even when they may not be able to make the decision.

## Summary

- Children and Families Act 2014 places emphasis on education professionals working with the young person and their parent to enable the young person make a successful transition to adulthood.

- Communication is at the heart of working effectively and supporting parents.

- Education professionals may need guidance and training in working with parents.

- To work effectively and support parents, education professionals need to be secure in their knowledge of the MCA.

- Education professionals should share strategies and approaches to facilitating decision-making with parents.

*Epilogue*

# Putting the MCA Principles and Processes into Practice
## Food for Thought

The Children and Families Act 2014 and Mental Capacity Act (MCA) 2005 share a common principle in encouraging a young person's participation in decision-making. The MCA is all about decision-making. The MCA Code of Practice (MCA COP) offers some practical suggestions about facilitating a person's decision-making, and most are well known to educationalists and already part of practice. The Special Educational Needs and Disability Code of Practice (SEND COP) highlights the need to involve young people in decision-making as fully as possible from a young age, but offers no guidance on how this can be achieved.

This book has explained the MCA principles and processes; the next step is for education professionals to integrate these into everyday practice. Although every individual education professional has a responsibility to ensure they follow the MCA principles, there is an onus on organisations to have policies and protocols in place. Therefore, educational establishments, local authority special educational needs (SEN) and personal budget sections ought to have appropriate policies and procedures in place.

### Developing a young person's ability to make decisions about their education

Fundamental to this is the education professional's basic understanding about making decisions and a belief in their own ability to make reasoned choices. A friend of the author's repeatedly says she is no good at making decisions, yet runs a successful business.

188     More often than not, we are unaware of how we are actually making a decision, as the process is routine. To teach decision-making, the education professional needs to be aware of the process. Think about a recent decision, perhaps booking a holiday, buying a new outfit, choosing a sandwich for lunch – now write down the process you went through to make the choice. Hopefully, this closely resembles the procedure described below.

The decision-making process begins with identifying the decision that needs to be made; this may include why the decision needs to be made and if there is a time limit. For example, choosing a new educational placement may be necessitated by the young person reaching the final year of their current one, and so choosing a new placement will need to be done within the local authority's time frame. The next step is to establish the options, work out what information is required and how this will be obtained – consider if there is anyone else who could assist. Using a grid such as the 'best interests' balance sheet may assist the young person analysing the pros and cons of each choice.

Some young people may absorb the decision-making process incidentally; others may require more explicit guidance. Young people with SEN will most likely require direct teaching, suggesting decision-making should be an outcome written into an Education, Health and Care (EHC) Plan.

There are some decisions that all young people will need to make at some point, such as choosing the next educational establishment. A young person's decision-making ability may be assisted by local authorities, or educational establishments, having a programme or protocol that ensures the young person obtains all the relevant information. Young people with SEN, who are the subject of EHC Plans, have additional challenges in understanding all the relevant information for some educational decisions as it entails demonstrating an awareness of abstract concepts, for example, the 'local authority'.

## Decision-making: EHC Plan outcomes

Should local authorities have a policy about writing decision-making into an EHC Plan? Probably, as this will legitimatise decision-making as a valid educational activity and facilitate young people's independence, in keeping with a SEND COP core principle. However, this raises a number of questions as outcomes have achievement dates. When should decision-making be written into the EHC Plan as an outcome – from the outset, at secondary transfer, or as an amendment following the Year 9 (Y9) annual review? By what age is it envisaged a young person will be able to make their own decisions – 16, 18 or 25?

If a decision-making outcome becomes policy in EHC Plans, this will probably generate the development of approaches and resources to support it, as well as prompting educational psychologists (EPs), particularly trainee EPs, to research and evaluate strategies. This would be to the young person's benefit.

## EHC Plans and the local authority's role

A young person who is the subject of an EHC Plan has to make decisions about its content annually. To be considered to have capacity to make a decision, the young person will probably have to demonstrate an awareness of the local authority's role in maintaining the EHC Plan. How practically can this be achieved? What steps would be written into a person-centred plan to enable a young person to develop this knowledge?

The starting point has to be introducing the young person to the idea of their EHC Plan. Although this may now be an electronic document, it can be printed out so that the young person can see it and touch it. The young person also needs a simple explanation about its content. Ideally, the young person will learn to recognise this document as it may be a key to helping them understand the abstract concept of the local authority. Some young people may require repeated, regular practice to learn to recognise the document. For visually impaired young people the document may need to be represented by a particular texture or smell.

Explaining that the local authority manages this document will probably be more challenging. However, linking the EHC Plan the young person recognises with an embodiment of the local authority may facilitate their understanding. This process may take a long time, requiring regular, repeated practice; ideally, it should become an outcome in a person-centred plan and, perhaps, an EHC Plan. The importance of trying to help the young person comprehend the idea of the local authority looking after their EHC Plan cannot be over-emphasised. For the young person, this could be the difference between being deemed to have or to lack capacity to make a particular educational decision.

### *Choosing a new educational establishment*

The local authority or educational establishment may wish to develop a programme and resources (electronic or paper) that support young people's preparation to make this choice. Basing this on the information a young person has to demonstrate in a capacity assessment would be most helpful. This includes knowing which educational establishments are being considered, what the young person likes and dislikes about the choices, and how they will travel to the establishments. This would enable a systematic collection of the information and may provide a focus for visits to the establishments.

### **…and finally**

Internet searches do reveal reports and articles by respected bodies, for example, the Care Quality Commission, that are critical of the implementation of the MCA since 2007, and much relates to use of the Deprivation of Liberty Safeguards (DoLS). These reports predate the March 2014 Supreme Court case giving a new definition and the subsequent Law Society guidance (2015). Brown and Marchant (2013) looked at the way practitioners with people with learning disabilities, in cases perceived as complex, applied the MCA. They noted that practitioners found it challenging using the clear decision-making framework, set out in the MCA and MCA COP, in real-life situations, finding some decisions did not fit into the model.

No legislation is perfect, or always easy to apply. This book began with a criticisms of the SEND COP Annex 1, so it is unsurprising that there are concerns about the MCA and MCA COP. Nonetheless, the MCA and its accompanying code of practice safeguards vulnerable young people's right to make their own decisions about what happens to them. However imperfectly an education professional may feel they have utilised the MCA principles, by trying to do so, they will have enabled a young person to make their own decision. If the young person lacks capacity to make the particular decision, by applying the MCA principles, perhaps through a capacity assessment, the education professional will have provided the young person with the opportunity to make known their views, wishes and feelings about the choice. Passing these to the parent, or representative, to consider when making a 'best interests' decision continues to support the young person having their views valued and a choice made that, hopefully, is the one they would have made themselves; perhaps realising the aspiration 'no decision about my education, without me' for this young person.

# Glossary

| | |
|---|---|
| **Assessor** | The person who does the capacity assessment with a young person who is thought to lack capacity to make the particular decision. For educational decisions this may be a member of school or college staff, or a local authority officer. |
| **'Best interests'** | Any decisions made, or anything done for a young person who lacks capacity to make specific decisions, must be in the young person's 'best interests'. |
| **'Best interests' checklist** | The checklist of things that whoever is making a particular decision on behalf of a young person who lacks capacity to make the decision must follow. It is set out in Chapter 5 of the Mental Capacity Act 2005 Code of Practice. |
| **Capacity assessment** | The two-stage assessment, set out in Chapter 4 of the Mental Capacity Act 2005 Code of Practice, which is undertaken when it is believed a young person lacks capacity to make a particular decision. |
| **Children and Families Act 2014** | The law that covers educational provision for children and young people in England with special educational needs and disabilities. |
| **Code of Practice (COP)** | A code of practice is the guidance that the government publishes about how a particular law should work on a day-to-day basis. It explains in more detail what the law means and gives practical steps. People in certain roles or jobs have to follow a particular COP; these roles or jobs are set out in the COP. |
| **Compulsory school age** | The beginning of the term following a child's fifth birthday until the last Friday in June in the school year in which the young person becomes 16. |

| | | |
|---|---|---|
| **Court of Protection** | | This is a specialist court for all issues relating to people who lack capacity to make a specific decision (see also the Resources section). |
| **Decision-maker** | | The person making a particular decision on behalf of a young person who has been assessed as lacking capacity to make the particular decision. For decisions relating to the young person's education, the decision-maker will generally be the young person's parent (Special Educational Needs and Disability Code of Practice Annex 1). |
| **Deprivation of liberty** | | The young person is under continuous supervision and control and is not free to leave and lacks capacity to consent to these arrangements. |
| **Education, Health and Care Plan (EHC Plan)** | | An EHC Plan details the education, health and social care support that is to be provided to a young person who has special educational needs or a disability. It is drawn up by the local authority after an education, health and care needs assessment of the young person has determined that an EHC Plan is necessary, and after consultation with partner agencies (SEND COP Chapter 9). |
| **EP** | | Educational psychologist. |
| **Further education (FE) (college)** | | A college offering continuing education to young people over the compulsory school age of 16. The FE sector in England includes general FE colleges, sixth form colleges, specialist colleges and adult education institutes. |
| **Lack capacity** | | A young person is considered to lack capacity if they have an impairment of, or a disturbance in the functioning of, their mind or brain and this affects their ability to make the specific decision at the time the decision is needed. This means the young person has learning difficulties or a learning disability, or difficulties with their emotional well-being or mental health issues and this affects their ability to make the specific decision when it is needed. |
| **Local Offer** | | Local authorities in England are required to set out provision they expect to be available across education, health and social care for children and young people in their area who have special education needs or who are disabled, including those who do not have Education, Health and Care Plans. |

| | |
|---|---|
| Mental capacity | The ability to make a decision – any decision, big or small. |
| Mental Capacity Act (MCA) 2005 | This law is about people making decisions for themselves. It assumes that everyone can make their own decisions until it is proved that they are not able to do so. It provides a statutory framework for people who lack capacity to make decisions for themselves. It sets out how decisions should be taken on behalf of someone who lacks capacity to make the decision. |
| Parent | Any person who is the young person's parent or who has parental responsibility or who cares for the young person. |
| Personal budget | A personal budget is an amount of money identified by the local authority to deliver provision set out in an Education, Health and Care Plan where the parent or young person is involved in securing that provision (Special Educational Needs and Disability Code of Practice 9.95). |
| SEN | Special educational needs. |
| Special Education Needs and Disability (SEND) Tribunal | First-tier SEND Tribunal, sometimes referred to as SENDIST or SEND Tribunal. It is part of Her Majesty's Courts and Tribunals Service. It is independent of the local authority. It determines appeals lodged by parents or a young person against a local authority's decisions in relation to an education, health and care needs assessments and the content of Education, Health and Care Plan Sections B, F and I. The Tribunal's decision is binding on both the parent or young person and the local authority. |
| Service user | The term used to refer to the clients of social workers and health professionals. In this book, it refers to a young person. |
| Young person | Someone aged 16–25. However, the definition in the Special Educational Needs and Disability Code of Practice is someone who has reached the end of Y11 (after the last Friday in June) and is 16 years old. |

*Appendix 1*

# Capacity Assessment Record Form

## Mental Capacity Act capacity assessment guidance notes

Please read these guidance notes carefully before undertaking a capacity assessment.

### *Preface*

A mental capacity assessment is *confidential*; the completed form should not be circulated generally, for example, as part of annual review paperwork.

Who receives a completed assessment form depends on the outcome of the assessment.

If the young person *has capacity*, they are given a copy of the completed form, and further copies are given to the person who needed the decision to be made and the young person's file. The young person's parent(s) can only be given a copy of the completed assessment with the young person's permission.

If the young person *lacks capacity* to make this decision, a copy of the completed assessment form should be given to the:

- young person
- person who needed the decision to be made
- young person's parent or representative as they will be making the decision on behalf of the young person
- young person's file.

## Introduction

This form, the MCA capacity assessment record (MCAcar), sets out the process to follow to undertake a capacity assessment when a young person needs to make a 'more serious or significant' or 'legal consequences' decision about their education, if there is a concern that the young person may not be able to do this.

The form should be used to record the capacity assessment. It is completed by the person undertaking the assessment – the assessor. Who the assessor is will depend on the nature of the decision. It is important that the assessor is identified when it is known that the young person will need to make the specific decision. The assessor will need to know who will make the decision on the young person's behalf if they lack capacity. For educational decisions, this will generally be the young person's parents or representative.

## Two-stage capacity assessment

A capacity assessment has two stages in the form of questions to be answered. Stage 1 determines whether a capacity assessment is required for this decision. Stage 2 is answered by using the 'four key questions' to determine whether the young person has, or lacks, capacity to make this particular decision.

### Stage 1

- *Does the young person have an impairment of, or a disturbance in the functioning of, their mind or brain?*
- **Does the young person have learning difficulties or learning disability, or difficulties with their emotional wellbeing or mental health issues?**

*Learning difficulty or learning disability:* the young person has a significantly reduced ability to understand new, or complex, information or to learn new skills, with a reduced ability to cope independently, which started before adulthood.

*Emotional wellbeing or mental health issues* relate to:

- depression
- anxiety: generalised anxiety, panic disorder, habit disorders such as obsessive-compulsive disorder, phobias and post-traumatic stress disorder
- bipolar disorder
- psychotic disorders, for example, schizophrenia
- hyperkinetic disorders: disturbance of activity and attention, for example, ADHD
    - mental and behavioural disorders caused by psychoactive substance misuse, for example, cannabis
    - eating disorders
    - autism
    - personality and behavioural changes caused by brain injury
    - deliberate self-harm.

If the answer to this question is *Yes*, go to *Stage 2*.

If the answer to this question is *No*, the young person has capacity to make this particular decision and no further action is necessary. In this circumstance, a capacity assessment *must not be undertaken* for this decision.

## Stage 2

- *Does the impairment or disturbance mean that the young person is unable to make a specific decision when they need to?*

- **Does the young person's learning difficulty or learning disability, emotional wellbeing difficulties or mental health issues mean that the young person is unable to make a specific decision when they need to?**

If the answer to this question is *Yes* or *Not sure*, a capacity assessment using the 'four key questions' should be undertaken.

If the answer to this question is *No*, the young person has capacity to make this particular decision and *no further action is necessary*.

### Capacity assessment using the 'four key questions'

1. Can the young person understand the information *relevant* to the decision, including understanding the consequences of not making the decision?

The young person needs to demonstrate:

- a basic understanding of the key points, not all the fine details
- that they know what decision has to made
- the reason why the decision has to be made
- an understanding that choosing one thing over another means they will not doing or going to the other choice(s)
- key points relating to the specific decision.

## 2. Can they retain the information long enough to make the decision?

In keeping with the second principle of the MCA, the young person must be given all the help and support necessary to facilitate them making this decision. This includes visual supports and any other materials that help them retain the information. A capacity assessment is not a test or exam.

## 3. Can they use and weigh the information to arrive at a choice?

This is about the young person being able to identify what they think is good or not good, or what they like or dislike about the choice(s) and having done so then make their choice.

## 4. Can they communicate their decision in any way?

The young person can use any verbal or non-verbal means of communicating their choice. The onus is on the assessor to be sure that they can understand the young person's means of communication.

## Outcome of the capacity assessment

If the answer to *one or more* of the 'four key questions' is 'No', on the balance of probabilities, the young person lacks capacity to make this decision at this time.

If the assessor is uncertain about the outcome of a capacity assessment, it should be repeated a few days later. If a repeated capacity assessment is felt to be unreliable, it will need to be repeated a third time.

# Capacity assessment process flow chart

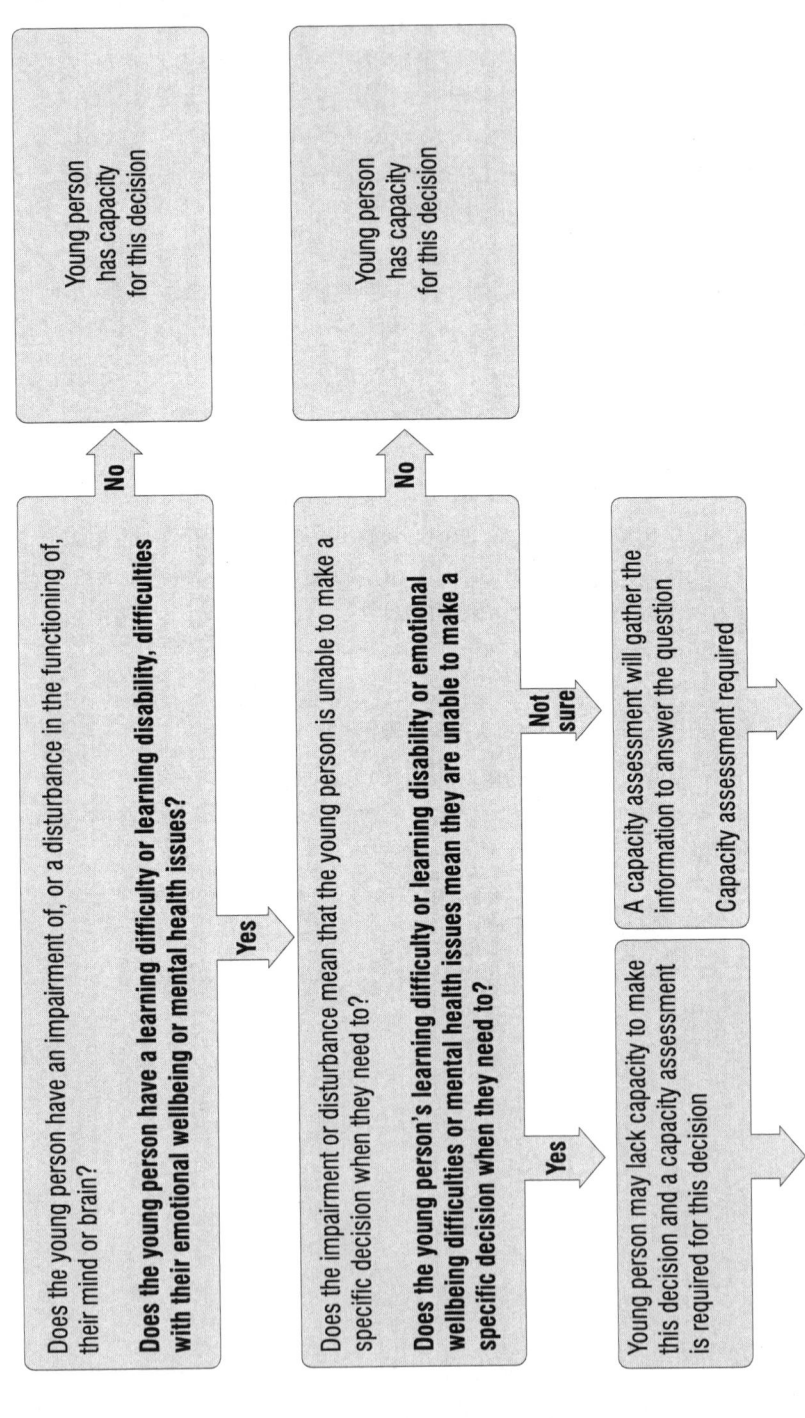

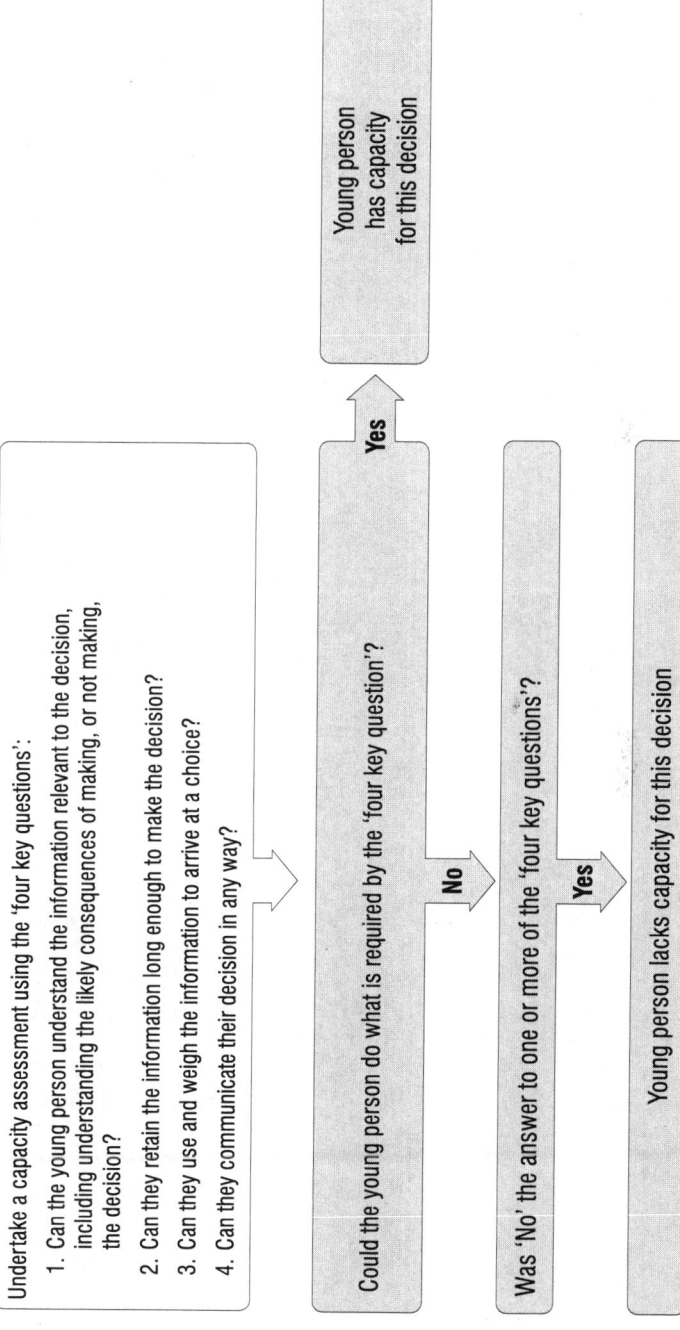

## Mental Capacity Act 2005 Capacity Assessment Record (MCAcar)

| Young person's details ||
|---|---|
| **Full name:** Jill Carmel Walsh | **Date of birth:** 03/06/1997 |
| **Address:**<br>9 Gentry Heights, Newtown<br>Bramblewick BK9 3LP | **EHC Plan:**<br><br>Yes ☑    No ☐ |
| **School UPN/College ID No.:** D000040010275<br><br>**School:** Old Town Special School<br><br>**Address:** Foundry Lane, Old Town, Bramblewick BK3 7BS ||
| **Date of the assessment:**<br><br>**Time of the assessment:** | 01/12/2015<br><br>**Start:** 10am    **Finish:** 11.45am |
| **Location of the assessment:** | Mr Singh's office |
| **Who else was present?** | Ms Attar, post-16 support assistant |
| **Does the young person have a sensory impairment?** | HI ☐    VI ☐    MSI ☐ |
| **How does the young person communicate?** | Makaton, some single words, not always intelligible. Sometimes uses her iPad to assist communication |

| Assessor's details ||
|---|---|
| **Full name:** Mrs Mary Wilson | **In what capacity do you know the young person?**<br>Year 14 class teacher |
| **Job title:** Post-16 teacher ||

## Capacity Assessment Record Form

| | |
|---|---|
| **Organisation:** Old Town Special School | **How long have you known the young person?** Since Jill joined the school in September 2008 |
| **Email:** vwilson@oldtown.org.uk | |
| **Phone number:** 0734 234566 | |
| I, the assessor, confirm that I have read and followed the guidance notes when completing this form: | Yes ☑   No ☐ |

| | |
|---|---|
| **Give details of anyone else consulted to make this assessment, e.g., speech and language therapist, educational psychologist, young person's teacher, key worker (teaching assistant), social worker, child psychiatrist, specialist teachers, etc.** | Mr Singh, Year 14 class teacher<br>Mrs Jones, life skills tutor, City Further Education college<br>Ms Patel, speech and language therapist. |

**Decision required:** Give full details.

Jill is in her final year at the special school so she has to choose her next educational placement. There are two FE colleges within the local authority area, although generally it is expected that the young person will attend the nearest one. Both offer a life skills course; they both offer options in animal care, but only one in 'fashion, hair and beauty'. Mrs Walsh, Jill's mother, has discussed with Jill about going away to college; her brother is away at university so Jill knows about leaving home to study and returning in the holidays. Jill does not want to leave home, so Mrs Walsh has suggested a residential placement is not included in the choices. Therefore, Jill's choice is between City FE College and Castle FE College.

**When does young person need to make the decision?**
*Is there a specific date or period of time for this decision?*

The local authority needs to have FE choices by 15 January 2016.

| | |
|---|---|
| **Who is concerned the young person may lack the capacity to make this decision?** |
| Mrs Walsh, Jill's mother |
| Mrs Jones, life skills tutor, City FE College |
| **What are the reasons for the concern the young person may lack the capacity to make this decision?** |
| Mrs Walsh does not think Jill understands the implications of choosing one way or the other and thinks she will choose the one her 'boyfriend' will be attending. |
| Mrs Jones is not sure about Jill's decision-making; her experience of Jill over the past two years is that she gives the answer she thinks will please whoever is asking her the question. In college, Jill has given different answers to different staff members when asked to select an activity. Also, she is not sure Jill understands about choosing something that will happen in the future. On the other hand, if Jill really wants to do something she does remember this, even if it is going to take place in the future. Mrs Jones does not think Jill will understand that when she has made her choice, the local authority have to agree with this. |
| **Is the young person aware that you are assessing their capacity to make this decision?** |
| No |
| **If the young person is found to lack capacity to make this decision, who will make the decision on their behalf?** *(Name of the person and their relationship to the young person. For decisions about the young person's education this will be the young person's parent or representative)* |
| Mrs Carmel Walsh, Jill's mother, and Mr Tony Selby, Jill's step-father |

## Capacity assessment

### Stage 1

*Does the young person have an impairment of, or disturbance in the functioning of, their mind or brain?*

**Does the young person have learning difficulties or learning disability, or difficulties with their emotional wellbeing or mental health issues?**

Yes ☑   No ☐

**If 'Yes': identify and set out all the young person's special educational needs and/or disabilities including their emotional wellbeing or mental health.** (It is not necessary for the young person to have been given a formal label for their difficulties, but if they do have one note it here.) *Note which of these are temporary or fluctuating.*

Jill has a life-long learning disability. She was slow to meet the early developmental milestones such as walking, talking and cognitive skills. Her understanding is generally in the here and now and about concrete things, probably at the level of the average five- to six-year-old. She has a very limited understanding of abstract concepts; sometimes if she has experienced it, she may show a basic comprehension. She learns very slowly, although she did master the iPad more quickly than expected. Jill's understanding of the social world is at the level of the average five-year-old, although she demonstrates more understanding when it comes to fashion and beauty, probably like an eight- to nine-year-old. In some social situations she can become confused about expectations; however, she is able to conduct herself socially appropriately in the college cafeteria and in school she helps with the younger pupils in the dining room.

Jill has very limited verbal communication; she has a very restricted single-word vocabulary. Since attending the FE college, she has added some new words to her vocabulary. Her speech varies in intelligibility depending on the speech sounds making up the word and her interest in communicating. She can use about 20 Makaton signs to supplement her oral communication. Sometimes this can assist the listener to understand her communication. School staff, along with her mother, are the most proficient at interpreting Jill's communication. Jill has been attending college for a day a week for the past two years, but college is still adjusting to her communication style. Although Jill likes animals and enjoys looking after them, she does not fully understand that they have the potential to hurt her.

Generally Jill seems happy, but it is noticeable when she is unhappy about something. Occasionally her unhappy state can last for a few days; usually it is more short-lived. Mostly, either school staff or her parents are aware of what has upset her. However, when she is upset it is much more difficult to engage her and she becomes a reluctant communicator.

### Stage 2

*Does the impairment or disturbance mean that the young person is unable to make a specific decision when they need to?*

**Does the young person's learning difficulty or learning disability, emotional wellbeing difficulties or mental health issues mean that the young person is unable to make a specific decision when they need to?**

Yes ☐     No ☐     Not sure ☑

If the answer to **Stage 1** is *No*, the young person *has capacity* and no further action needed.

If the answer to **Stage 1** is *Yes* and the answer to **Stage 2** is *Yes* or *Not sure*, continue to the *capacity assessment using the 'four key questions'.*

Capacity Assessment Record Form

# 'Four key questions'

### 1. Can the young person understand basic, relevant information relating to the decision to be made?

*What did the young person say or do in relation to:*

- *The decision to be made*

Jill was aware that she had to pick a college; she recognised the photos of the two colleges and used her Makaton signs for each one. She has been using the sign for 'bird' for City College as the coat of arms over the main entrance has owls on it. Her way of saying Castle College was the Makaton sign for 'sandcastle' as the depiction of a castle in the college literature resembles a sandcastle. She could point to the City College photo when asked which one she goes to with school.

- *The reason the decision is needed*

Jill knew that she was in the top class at school and there were no more classes. She demonstrated she knew this meant she had to leave school.

- *Showing they know what choosing one thing over another means will happen*

Jill seemed confused about the idea of only going to one place. Perhaps this was because, for the past two years, she has been attending school and college. She knew that City College has an animal care option, but she also wants to do 'fashion, hair and beauty', which is not offered there. She thought she could go to the other college to do that. She seemed to want to go to City College, possibly because she knows it, rather than a considered choice.

- *Key facts about the specific choices (Give details)*

**City College**

Jill demonstrated that she was aware that:

- she could do animal care, but not 'fashion, hair and beauty'
- the bus stop to college is near her home and it stops outside college
- she will travel in a minibus until she learns how to use the bus
- the cafeteria has nice food
- she can go to the cafeteria by herself
- she has friends there; she named a couple of students that help in the life skills area
- students go out in the minibus
- sometimes students cook their own lunch
- she will do work experience
- her 'boyfriend' is choosing this college
- Mrs Jones will help her with her work
- using iPads in lessons
- Jill did not know that horticulture is the second option offered at the college

**Castle College**

Jill demonstrated that she was aware that:

- she could do animal care and 'fashion, hair and beauty'
- the bus stops near her home. Jill thinks the college is a long way from her house
- she saw the cafeteria when she visited, but she does not know if the food is nice
- she will get help with the work, but she does not know who will help her
- using iPad in lessons
- she can do work experience in a hairdressers
- college has a hairdressing and beauty room
- sometimes students cook their own lunch
- students go on a visit and sleep there

Jill was unable to demonstrate that she was aware the local authority would have to agree her choice.

Is the young person able to demonstrate that they are aware of:

- the decision they need to make?  Yes ☑  No ☐
- the reason the decision is needed?  Yes ☑  No ☐
- choosing one thing over another means they will not be doing or going to the other choice(s)?  Yes ☐  No ☑
- the key facts about the decision?  Yes ☑  No ☐
- the local authority needing to agree their choice?  Yes ☐  No ☑

## What information has the young person been given?

### City College

Jill has been attending the college on a weekly basis for two years. She is familiar with key places in the building and some staff. In preparation, school staff and her parents talked to her about what the college offers, in particular the options and practical activities. Jill took photos on her iPad of relevant places and key staff. She was videoed doing some activities at college. Jill talked to Mrs Jones, her college tutor, about what would be on offer. Jill had the photos, video recordings on her iPad and she looked at these with school staff and her parents. Jill's mother took Jill on the bus from home to college on a couple of occasions. Jill photographed the main entrance with the nameplate. Mrs Jones used Jill's iPad to make a folder of pictures of the five most important things about studying at City College: animal care and horticulture options, using iPads in lessons, students cooking their own lunch, having help with learning and going out in the minibus.

### Castle College

Jill visited the college three times, twice with her mother and once with Mrs Wilson. Jill was shown all the key places that the life skills students use during the course of a week. She was shown the cafeteria, toilets, main office and library. She talked with Mrs Ahmed, a tutor, about what would be offered, in particular options and practical activities. Mrs Darcy, the learning assistant, showed Jill around the life skills department. On one visit, Jill joined in a cookery lesson; she was supported by Mrs Darcy, who took photos of Jill doing the activity. Jill photographed the main entrance with the nameplate. Mrs Ahmed used Jill's iPad to make a folder of pictures of the five most important things about studying at Castle College: animal care and 'fashion, hair and beauty' options, using iPads in lessons, having help with learning, students cooking their own lunch and the annual residential trip.

Prior to the visits school staff had worked with Jill using the school's 'choosing a college' materials, so Jill was aware of what to look for, such as where lunch is eaten, the location of the toilets, as well as what she would learn.

Additionally, school staff worked with Jill during Years 12 and 13 to try to teach her to understand the concept of the local authority and its role looking after her EHC Plan. School staff used a photo of Ms Joseph, local authority SEN officer, with her cat brooch, holding Jill's EHC Plan to represent the local authority. Ms Joseph attended Jill's Year 13 annual review and she has seen Jill on other visits to the school. Jill now recognises Ms Joseph, and knows that she works in an office. Jill recognises her EHC Plan, but she has been unable to grasp the idea of the local authority or its role in managing the EHC Plan. During the assessment Jill was shown the Ms Joseph photo but other than recognising her Jill could not demonstrate she knew that the local authority would have to agree with her college choice.

**How was the information given?**
*(e.g., in large print, sign language, braille, pictures, easy read, large print, via a visual medium such as DVD, etc.)*

Jill visited both colleges, she took photos, and videos were made of her during the visits taking part in activities. College staff photographed and videoed the five most important things about attending the college. School staff and her parents talked to Jill using the materials about choosing which college to attend. Jill chose her own Makaton signs for the two options; school staff and her parents used these with her when talking with her about the choices.

The photo of Ms Joseph holding Jill's EHC Plan to represent the local authority.

### 2. Can the young person retain the information long enough to make the decision?

Yes ☑    No ☐

**What memory aids was the young person helped to use to assist them?** *(e.g. photographs, audio or visual recordings, pictures, etc.)*

All the photos and videos recorded on Jill's iPad were used during the assessment, as well as the photo Jill had taken of the main entrance of each college with its nameplate. These had been printed to use as a prompt to ensure Jill knew to which college the questions referred and allowed her to put smiley and sad faces under on photos under each college when she was asked specific things about each college related to the five most important things identified by the college staff. At the end, there was a visual record of Jill's views, which was photographed so Ms Joseph and Jill's mother would be made aware of her views. This would assist Jill's mother in taking Jill's wishes and feelings into consideration when she was making the decision on Jill's behalf in Jill's 'best interests'.

In addition, Ms Joseph's photo was displayed throughout the assessment.

**How do you know the young person has retained the information?** *(give details with examples)*

Jill was able to recognise the photo of each college and the photos of the five most important things about each college. She could talk about the bus journey to each college. Overall, she recognised more photos and information related to City College than Castle College. At the end of the session, Jill was asked to identify each photo to ensure she still recalled what it represented.

Jill recognised Ms Joseph's photo; she knew she worked in an office. She was amused that Ms Joseph was holding Jill's EHC Plan. Jill was unable to show any understanding that Ms Joseph manages Jill's EHC Plan.

## 3. Can the young person this information to arrive at a decision?

Yes ☐    No ☒

**How do you know that the young person used the information to arrive at their decision?**

Jill recognised both colleges. She thought the animal care option was good for both; 'fashion, hair and beauty' was a good point about Castle College. However, she did not seem able to grasp that she had to choose one college to attend. She wanted to go to City College because she likes it, probably because she has been going there for two years, and her 'boyfriend' was going there; this was likely as he lives in the local authority's catchment area for this college, as does Jill. She wants to do 'fashion, hair and beauty', and kept saying she could go to the other college to do this.

**How are you sure that this is the young person's own decision and not one to please others, or because they have been influenced in any way by anyone?**

Jill's apparent preference for City College is probably related to familiarity, having attended there a day a week for two years. It took Jill a long time to get used to the college, but she is now comfortable in college. She can find her own way to the cafeteria and toilets unaccompanied. Although Jill could indicate what she liked and disliked about the two colleges, she could not grasp she could only choose one. There was no suggestion that Jill's choice was influenced by factors other than her own views.

### 4. Can the young person communicate their decision by any means?

Yes ☑  No ☐

#### How did the young person communicate their decision?

Jill used the Makaton sign she had been using for City College – bird – and pointed to the photograph. Then she pointed to Castle College and made the Makaton sign for 'sandcastle'. It was then explained that she had to choose just one college, yet again she pointed to both.

#### What did they communicate about the choices?

During the course of the assessment Jill indicated her likes and dislikes about each college using smiley and sad faces that she put on the five most important things about the college prepared by the tutors from the respective colleges. Jill put smiley faces for both colleges on using an iPad for learning, having help and students cooking their own lunch. She put a smiley face on the 'fashion, hair and beauty' option at Castle College and a sad face on the 'horticulture' option at City College. She also put a sad face on the 'annual residential' trip photo for Castle College and a smiley face on the minibus trips at City College. Over the course of the assessment Jill made more positive comments about City College than Castle College.

*What the young person has communicated can be considered as an indication of their wishes and feelings about this matter, if they are considered to lack capacity to make this decision. The young person's parent/representative should give consideration to the wishes and feelings of the young person to assist them in making the decision in the young person's 'best interests'.*

## Attach any relevant documents

#### Any additional comments

Jill seemed happy and comfortable during the assessment. She engaged well with the session. There was nothing to suggest there were any physical or emotional factors that may affect the outcome. Jill's mother had confirmed that, as far as she was aware, Jill was fine.

Capacity Assessment Record Form

### Outcome of the assessment

*If the answer to any of the questions 1–4 is 'No', the young person lacks capacity to make this decision at this time.*

On the balance of probabilities,

_____ has the capacity to make this decision at this time. ☐

Jill Carmel Walsh does not have the capacity to make this decision at this time. ☑

| | |
|---|---|
| **Assessor's signature:** | *Mary Wilson* |
| **Full name:** | Mrs Mary Wilson |
| **Job title:** | Post-16 teacher |
| **Date:** | 1 December 2015 |

## Copies

| If the young person *lacks capacity*: | If the young person *has capacity*: |
|---|---|
| File | File |
| Young person | Young person |
| Parent/representative | |
| Person who needed the decision to be made | |

## CAPACITY ASSESSMENT GROUND RULES

 Switch off mobile phones unless they are needed to assist the young person's communication

  Let the young person communicate for themselves, even if it takes them time to give a response

 Be patient, this process takes time

 Reassure the young person there are no wrong answers

  Give the young person encouragement to respond

 The assessment is confidential

*Appendix 2*

# Identifying Which Young People May Be Considered to Lack Capacity

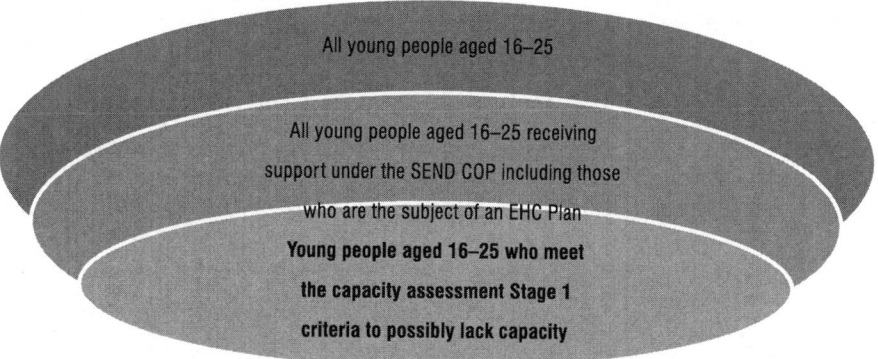

**Figure A2.1** Diagram showing that not all young people receiving support under the SEND COP will meet the criteria to be considered to possibly lack capacity

The diagram shows that it is only a small number of young people who are receiving support under the SEND COP, including those who are the subject of an EHC Plan, will meet the MCA COP Stage 1 capacity assessment criteria for it to be considered they may lack capacity to make a particular decision. Being the subject of an EHC Plan has no bearing on a young person's capacity to make a particular decision.

The young people who are more likely to have difficulties making decisions are likely either to be attending educational establishments or courses catering for those with significant learning disabilities or who have significant mental health problems and are receiving education or training from any type of post-16 education provider.

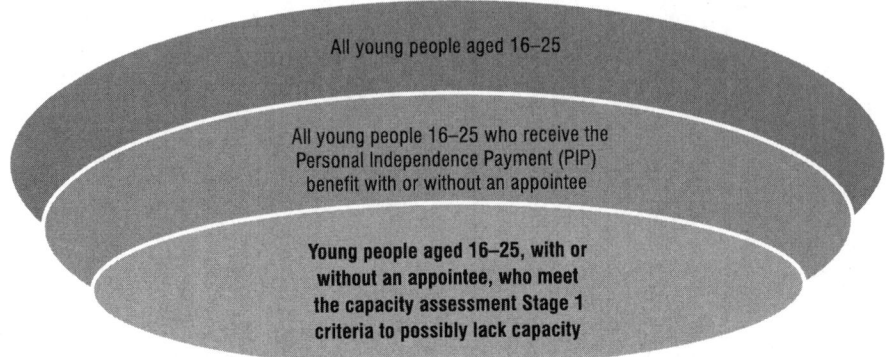

**Figure A2.2** Diagram showing that not all young people in receipt of the Personal Independent Payment benefit, and have an appointee, will meet the criteria to be considered to possibly lack capacity

The diagram shows that it is only a small number of young people who are in receipt of the Personal Independence Payment benefit, and have an appointee, will meet the MCA COP Stage 1 capacity assessment criteria for it to be considered they may lack capacity to make a particular decision. Having an appointee to manage the Personal Independence Payment benefit has no bearing on the young person's capacity to make decisions about their education. The appointee has to be approved by the Department for Work and Pensions (DWP) and is for managing the young person's benefits; their role does not extend to decision-making other areas of the young person's life.

*Appendix 3*

# 'Best Interests'

## Statutory 'best interests' checklist as set out in the Mental Capacity Act 2005 Code of Practice (Chapter 5, pp.65–66)

A person trying to work out the 'best interests' of a person who lacks capacity to make a particular decision ('lacks capacity') should:

### Encourage participation

- Do whatever is possible to permit and encourage the person to take part, or to improve their ability to take part, in making the decision.

### Identify all relevant circumstances

- Try to identify all the things that the person who lacks capacity would take into account if they were making the decision or acting for themselves.

### Find out the person's views

- Try to find out the views of the person who lacks capacity, including:
  - the person's past and present wishes and feelings – these may have been expressed verbally, in writing or through behaviour or habits

- any beliefs and values (for example, religious, cultural, moral or political) that would be likely to influence the decision in question
- any other factors the person themselves would be likely to consider if they were making the decision or acting for themselves.

## *Avoid discrimination*

- Do not make assumptions about someone's best interests simply on the basis of the person's age, appearance, condition or behaviour.

## *Assess whether the person might regain capacity*

- Consider whether the person is likely to regain capacity (for example, after receiving medical treatment). If so, can the decision wait until then?

## *If the decision concerns life-sustaining treatment*

- Do not be motivated in any way by a desire to bring about the person's death. They should not make assumptions about the person's quality of life.

## *Consult others*

- If it is practical and appropriate to do so, consult other people for their views about the person's best interests and to see if they have any information about the person's wishes and feelings, beliefs and values. In particular, try to consult:

- anyone previously named by the person as someone to be consulted on either the decision in question or on similar issues

- anyone engaged in caring for the person

- close relatives, friends or others who take an interest in the person's welfare

- any attorney appointed under a Lasting Power of Attorney or Enduring Power of Attorney made by the person

- any deputy appointed by the Court of Protection to make decisions for the person.

For decisions about major medical treatment or where the person should live and where there is no one who fits into any of the above categories, an independent mental capacity advocate (IMCA) must be consulted. (For more information about IMCAs, see the MCA COP Chapter 10.)

When consulting, remember that the person who lacks the capacity to make the decision or to act for him or herself still has a right to keep their affairs private – so it would not be right to share every piece of information with everyone.

## *Avoid restricting the person's rights*

- See if there are other options that may be less restrictive of the person's rights.

## *Take all of this into account*

- Weigh up all of these factors in order to work out what is in the person's 'best interests'.

## 'Best interests' checklist as written in the legislation
### Section 4: best interests

1. In determining for the purposes of this Act what is in a person's best interests, the person making the determination must not make it merely on the basis of:

    a) the person's age or appearance, or

    b) a condition of his, or an aspect of his behaviour, which might lead others to make unjustified assumptions about what might be in his best interests.

2. The person making the determination must consider all the relevant circumstances and, in particular, take the following steps.

3. He must consider:

    a) whether it is likely that the person will at some time have capacity in relation to the matter in question, and

    b) if it appears likely that he will, when that is likely to be.

4. He must, so far as reasonably practicable, permit and encourage the person to participate, or to improve his ability to participate, as fully as possible in any act done for him and any decision affecting him.

5. Where the determination relates to life-sustaining treatment he must not, in considering whether the treatment is in the best interests of the person concerned, be motivated by a desire to bring about his death.

6. He must consider, so far as is reasonably ascertainable:

    a) the person's past and present wishes and feelings (and, in particular, any relevant written statement made by him when he had capacity),

    b) the beliefs and values that would be likely to influence his decision if he had capacity, and

c) the other factors that he would be likely to consider if he were able to do so.

7. He must take into account, if it is practicable and appropriate to consult them, the views of:

   a) anyone named by the person as someone to be consulted on the matter in question or on matters of that kind,

   b) anyone engaged in caring for the person or interested in his welfare,

   c) any donee of a lasting power of attorney granted by the person, and

   d) any deputy appointed for the person by the court, as to what would be in the person's best interests and, in particular, as to the matters mentioned in subsection (6).

8. The duties imposed by subsections (1) to (7) also apply in relation to the exercise of any powers which:

   a) are exercisable under a lasting power of attorney, or

   b) are exercisable by a person under this Act where he reasonably believes that another person lacks capacity.

9. In the case of an act done, or a decision made, by a person other than the court, there is sufficient compliance with this section if (having complied with the requirements of subsections (1) to (7)) he reasonably believes that what he does or decides is in the best interests of the person concerned.

10. 'Life-sustaining treatment' means treatment which in the view of a person providing healthcare for the person concerned is necessary to sustain life.

11. 'Relevant circumstances' are those:

    a) of which the person making the determination is aware, and

    b) which it would be reasonable to regard as relevant.

## Sample completed 'best interests' balance sheets

**Young person's name:** Jill Carmel Walsh

**Name of person filling in the balance sheet:** Carmel Wilson (mother)

**Option 1:** City Further Education College for a life skills course with option choices of animal care or horticulture with work experience related to the chosen option.

| ✓☺ What would Jill like about this choice? | X☹ What would Jill not like about this choice? |
|---|---|
| Jill has already been attending one day a week and knows the staff. She knows her way around the part of the college associated with her course. She can find the cafeteria herself and buy her own sandwich. She likes Mrs Jones and Mr Malik. | Mrs Jones is retiring in the summer and Jill will have to get to know a new member of staff. Jill finds it hard getting to know new places and people. |
| She can learn about animal care, she likes animals and wants to work at her aunt's cattery. The college has indicated they would consider a work placement at her aunt's cattery or the city farm. | The animal care work experience placements are mainly at vet's practices and Jill does not like to see animals being hurt. Jill is also interested in hair, beauty and fashion, which are not options at this college. She has no experience of horticulture as the family do not have a garden. |
| She will be able to learn to travel to college by bus. The bus stop is near her home; the journey takes about 15 minutes and the bus stops very close to the college entrance. | She is worried about learning to travel independently and thinks she may be made to do this before she is ready. |
| The course is three years and she can stay at the college until she is 25 years old. | The college does not do riding for the disabled, which Jill enjoys. The students play badminton or go swimming. |
| Jill's best friend and 'boyfriend' are going to be attending this college. | Jill is worried about what will happen if she falls out with her 'boyfriend'. When they had an argument, she was unhappy going to school and seeing him, until a member of staff helped them resolve their differences. |

| There is a weekly trip out in the minibus. The places visited include the countryside, parks, the city farm, city centre and museums. | Jill is not keen on the countryside; she does not mind the park if she can feed the ducks. |

**Young person's name:** Jill Carmel Walsh

**Name of person filling in the balance sheet:** Carmel Walsh (mother)

**Option 2:** Castle Further Education College for a life skills course with option choices of animal care or personal care (fashion, hair, beauty) with work experience related to the chosen option.

| ✓☺ What would Jill like about this choice? | X ☹ What would Jill not like about this choice? |
|---|---|
| Over the three years of the course, Jill will be able to take both options, which are things that interest her. She likes doing her sister's hair. She is beginning to wear some make-up and likes to have fashionable clothes. She likes looking after animals and wants to work in her aunt's cattery. | Apart from a couple of visits, Jill does not know this college. It is further away from home, although there is a bus from near her home that stops close to the college. The journey takes about 30 minutes. |
| Jill does want to learn to travel independently. She does not mind walking to the bus stop on the main road for the bus to this college. | She is worried that she will be made to travel independently before she is really ready to do so. |
| The animal care work experience placements are at catteries, kennels and the city farm. | These are all close to the college rather than near her home. She would not be able to have a work experience placement at her aunt's cattery. |
| A couple of young people from Jill's school are going to this college, but she is not friendly with them at school. | Jill is worried she will miss her friend and 'boyfriend' if she does not see them every day at college. She is worried her 'boyfriend' will find someone else. |
| Jill can stay at the college until she is 25 years old. | |
| College has a residential visit each year, usually in the UK. | Jill thinks she will miss her parents and sister if she goes away. |

**Young person's name:** Jill Carmel Walsh

**Name of person filling in the balance sheet:** Carmel Walsh (mother)

**Option 1:** City Further Education College for a life skills course with option choices of animal care or horticulture with work experience related to the chosen option.

**Option 2:** Castle Further Education College for a life skills course with option choices of animal care or personal care (fashion, hair, beauty) with work experience related to the chosen option.

## *Discussion with school staff*

| Option 1 | Option 2 |
| --- | --- |
| Jill is very comfortable at college and can find her way round the part of the college used by the life skills students. It took her about six months to develop the confidence to find her way from one room to the next, and it is only recently that she will go to the cafeteria on her own to buy her sandwich at lunchtime. Jill has good relationships with all the staff and they know her well. | Jill's class teacher thinks Jill's friendships are very important to her, and that she would find it difficult being at a college without her best friend. They have been friends since Year 7. Going somewhere so unfamiliar may set her back for a whilst. |
| The options are limited and horticulture probably will not interest Jill. The college is thinking about expanding the options and work experience placements. | Jill would really enjoy the personal care and animal care options. |
| Jill is ready to learn to travel independently if the journey is relatively short. | A half-hour journey may be a bit long for Jill on her own and it may take a long time for her to develop the confidence to do this. |
| Jill really enjoys day or part day trips out in the minibus. | Jill would only go for one night of the three on the school residential trip to the local authority residential facility on the edge of the city. It is unlikely she would take part in the college residential. |

*Appendix 4*

# What Young People Can Legally Do from the Age of 16

At 16 years old a young person can:

- Armed Forces: join the army.

- Drinking alcohol:

    o  drink alcohol with a meal if in licensed premises if it is bought by an adult

    o  be given an alcoholic drink at home by their parents provided it is done responsibly.

- Driving:

    o  apply for a provisional licence aged 15 years 9 months

    o  drive a moped or light quad bike

    o  drive a car if they are in receipt of the enhanced rate for the mobility component of personal independence payments.

- Education: leave school, but must continue to participate in education or training, for example, apprenticeships, traineeships, supported internships, until the age of 18.

- Gambling: buy a lottery ticket.

- Leave home: leave home without their parents' permission.

- Marriage: get married with their parents' consent. If the young person's parents are married or were at the time of the young person's birth, both have to give consent. If the parents are not married, the parent with parental responsibility has to give their permission. If consent is not given, the young person can apply to the court for permission.

- Medical treatments:
    - consent to medical procedures
    - choose their own doctor
    - if they are female, buy emergency contraception from a pharmacy.
- Pet: buy a pet.
- Sex:
    - young people can consent to heterosexual sex with another person who is aged 16 or over
    - young people can consent to homosexual sex with another person who is aged 16 or over
    - anyone aged 18 years or over who is in a position of trust is not allowed to engage in sexual relations with a young person aged under the age of 18.
- Smoking: cannot buy tobacco products or smoke them.
- Work: work full time after the end of compulsory schooling, which is the last Friday in June in the school year in which the young person becomes 16. This is usually Year 11. Young people are automatically sent a National Insurance number when they become 16 years old.

# References

American Psychiatric Association (undated) *Warning Signs of Mental Health.* Available at www.psychiatry.org/mental-health/more-topics/warning-signs-of-mental-illness, accessed on 1 October 2015.

Atkinson, C., Dunsmuir, S., Lang, J. and Wright, S. (2015) 'Developing a competency framework for the initial training of educational psychologists working with young people aged 16 -25.' *Educational Psychology in Practice 31*, 2, 159–173.

British Psychological Society (2006) *Assessment of Capacity in Adults: Interim Guidance for Psychologists.* Leicester: British Psychological Society. Available at http://shop.bps.org.uk/assessment-of-capacity-in-adults-interim-guidance-for-psychologists.html, accessed on 1 October 2015.

British Psychological Society (2007) *Best Interests. Guidance in Determining the Best Interests of Adults Who Lack Capacity to Make a Decision (or Decisions) for Themselves. [England and Wales].* Leicester: British Psychological Society. Available at http://shop.bps.org.uk/best-interests-guidance-on-adults-who-lack-capacity-to-make-decisions-for-themselves-england-and-wales.html, accessed on 1 October 2015.

British Psychological Society and Royal College of Psychiatrists (2007) *Mental Capacity Act (2005): Short Reference Guide for Psychologists and Psychiatrists.* Leicester: British Psychological Society. Available at www.bps.org.uk/sites/default/files/documents/mental_capacity_act_2005_-_short_reference_guide_for_psychologists_and_psychiatrists.pdf, accessed on 1 October 2015.

British Psychological Society and Social Care Institute for Excellence (2010) *Audit Tool for Mental Capacity Assessments.* Leicester: British Psychological Society. Available at www.bps.org.uk/sites/default/files/documents/audit-tool-mental-capacity-assessments_0.pdf, accessed on 1 October 2015.

Brown, H. and Marchant, L. (2013) 'Using the Mental Capacity Act in complex cases.' *Tizard Learning Disability Review 18,* 2, 60–69.

Chief Medical Officer (2012) *Annual Report: Our Children Deserve Better Prevention*. Available at www.gov.uk/government/publications/chief-medical-officers-annual-report-2012-our-children-deserve-better-prevention-pays/cmos-annual-report-2012-our-children-deserve-better-cmos-summary-as-a-web-page#mental-health, accessed on 1 October 2015.

Council for Disabled Children (2014) *Information for Children and Young People on SEND Reforms, Videos*. London: Council for Disabled Children. Available at www.councilfordisabledchildren.org.uk/resources/information-for-children-and-young-people-on-send-reforms, accessed on 1 October 2015.

Department for Education (2013) *Section 139A: Learning Difficulty Assessments: Statutory Guidance For Local Authorities*. Available at www.gov.uk/government/publications/learning-difficulty-assessments, accessed on 1 October 2015.

Department for Education (2014) *Mental Health and Behaviour in Schools: Departmental Advice*. Available at www.gov.uk/government/publications/mental-health-and-behaviour-in-schools--2, accessed on 1 October 2015.

Department for Education and Department of Health (2015) *Special Educational Needs and Disability Code of Practice: 0–25 Years (January 2015)*. Available at www.gov.uk/government/uploads/system/uploads/attachment_data/file/398815/SEND_Code_of_Practice_January_2015.pdf, accessed on 1 October 2015.

Department of Health (2001) White Paper *Valuing People: A New Strategy for Learning Disability for the 21st Century*. Available at www.gov.uk/government/uploads/system/uploads/attachment_data/file/250877/5086.pdf, accessed on 1 October 2015.

Department of Health (2006) *Mental Capacity Act. Easy Read Summary*. Available at http://webarchive.nationalarchives.gov.uk/+/http://www.dca.gov.uk/menincap/mca-act-easyread.pdf, accessed on 1 October 2015.

Department of Health (2012) *Liberating the NHS: No Decision About Me, Without Me*. London: DH. Available at www.gov.uk/government/uploads/system/uploads/attachment_data/file/216980/Liberating-the-NHS-No-decision-about-me-without-me-Government-response.pdf, accessed on 1 October 2015.

Department of Health (2015) *Mental Health Act 1983 Code of Practice*. Available at www.gov.uk/government/uploads/system/uploads/attachment_data/file/396918/Code_of_Practice.pdf, accessed on 1 October 2015.

# References

Down's Syndrome Association (2014) *Mental Capacity Act 2005 and Code of Practice.* Available at www.downs-syndrome.org.uk/download-package/mental-capacity-act-2005-and-code-of-practice/, accessed on 1 October 2015.

Foundation for People with Learning Disabilities (2015) *A Guide to Circles of Support.* Available at www.learningdisabilities.org.uk/our-work/family-friends-community/circles-of-support/, accessed on 1 October 2015.

Fox, M. (2015) '"What sort of person ought I to be?" – Repositioning EPs in light of the Children and Families Bill (2013).' *Educational Psychology in Practice 31*, 4, 382–396

Headway (undated) www.headway.org.uk, accessed on 1 October 2015.

Law Society (2015) *Identifying a Deprivation of Liberty: A Practical Guide.* Available at www.lawsociety.org.uk/support-services/advice/articles/deprivation-of-liberty, accessed on 1 October 2015.

Mackay, M.A. and Murphy, J. (2012) *Talking Mats® and the World Health Organization International Classification of Functioning Disability and Health – Children and Youth. A Framework for Helping Adolescents Set IEP Targets.* Available at www.talkingmats.com/wp-content/uploads/2013/09/Talking-Mats-and-ICF-CY-Final-Report-Sep-2012.pdf, accessed on 1 October 2015.

Mantra Lingua Creative Learning for Diverse Classrooms (resources catalogue). Available at www.mantralingua.com, accessed on 9 November 2015.

MCA COP (2007) *Mental Capacity Act 2005: Code of Practice.* Available at www.gov.uk/government/uploads/system/uploads/attachment_data/file/224660/Mental_Capacity_Act_code_of_practice.pdf, accessed on 1 October 2015. Mencap (undated) *Mental Capacity Act Resource Pack.* Available at www.mencap.org.uk/sites/default/files/documents/mental capacity act resource pack.pdf, accessed on 1 October 2015.

Mental Health Foundation (undated) *Assessing Mental Capacity Audit Tool (AMCAT).* Available at www.amcat.org.uk, accessed on 1 October 2015.

Mitchell, W. (2012) 'Parents' accounts: factors considered when deciding how far to involve their son/daughter with learning disabilities in choice-making.' *Children and Youth Services Review 34*, 8, 1560–1569.

National Autistic Society (2007) *Moving On Up.* Available at www.autism.org.uk/about-autism/our-publications/reports/our-policy-and-research-reports/moving-on-up.aspx, accessed on 1 October 2015.

Oxford Reference (1981) *The Concise Oxford Dictionary of Quotations*. Oxford: Oxford University Press.

Preparing for Adulthood (2015) *Factsheet: The Mental Capacity Act 2005 and Supported Decision Making*. Available at http://preparingforadulthood.org.uk/resources/all-resources/pfa-factsheet-the-mental-capacity-act-2005-and-supported-decision-making, accessed on 1 October 2015.

Sinson, J. (2015) *No Decision About My Education Without Me. A Guide for Parents and Carers Helping Young People (16–25 Years) Make their Own Decisions about their Education*. London: National Sensory Impairment Partnership (NatSIP). Available at www.natsip.org.uk, accessed on 30 November 2015.

Supreme Court (2014) *P v. Cheshire West & Chester Council; P & Q v. Surrey County Council [2014] UKSC 19*. Available at www.supremecourt.uk/decided-cases/docs/UKSC_2012_0068_Judgment.pdf, accessed on 19 October 2015.

United Nations (undated) *Definition of Youth*. Available at www.un.org/esa/socdev/documents/youth/fact-sheets/youth-definition.pdf, accessed on 1 October 2015.

Walji, I., Fletcher, I. and Weatherhead, S. (2014) 'Clinical psychologists implementation of the Mental Capacity Act.' *Social Care and Neurodisability* 5, 2, 111–130.

Weare, K. (2015) *What Works in Promoting Social and Emotional Well-being and Responding to Mental Health Problems in Schools?* Available at www.ncb.org.uk/media/1197143/ncb_framework_for_promoting_well-being_and_responding_to_mental_health_in_schools.pdf, accessed on 1 October 2015.

Welsh Government (2015) *Draft Additional Learning Needs and Education Tribunal (Wales) Bill*. Available at http://gov.wales/consultations/education/draft-aln-and-education-tribunal-wales-bill/?lang=en, accessed on 1 October 2015.

# Resources

## Action on Hearing Loss

A charity that provides free confidential impartial advice to people who are deaf, their families, friends and professionals.

>   www.actiononhearingloss.org.uk

## BILD (British Institute of Learning Disabilities)

A charity that promotes the rights of people with learning disabilities to be valued equally, participate fully in their local communities and to be treated with dignity and respect. It offers training and other services to the organisations that provide services and the people who give support.

>   www.bild.org.uk

## Depression Alliance

A charity for anyone affected by depression. Provides support and information as well as campaigning to end the stigma of depression.

>   www.depressionalliance.org

## Department for Education (DfE)

(2015) Counselling in Schools: A Blueprint for the Future. Departmental Advice for School Leaders and Counsellors. March 2015.

>   www.gov.uk/government/uploads/system/uploads/attachment_data/file/416326/Counselling_in_schools_-240315.pdf

## Department for Education (DfE)

YouTube videos for young people about the SEND reforms.

www.youtube/user/educationgovuk

## Down's Syndrome Association

A charity that offers advice and information to people with Down's syndrome and their families.

www.downs-syndrome.org.uk

## HeadMeds

A Young Minds website providing information for young people about the 21 most common mental health medications and mental health conditions.

www.headmeds.org.uk

## Headway

The brain injury association website. Headway is a charity promoting understanding of all aspects of brain injury and provides information, support and services to survivors, their families and carers. It also campaigns to reduce the incidence of brain injury.

www.headway.org.uk

## Information, Advice & Support Services Network

Provides training and support to local Impartial information, advice & support services.

www.iassnetwork.org.uk

## Local Offer

Local authority website setting out what is available within the local authority across education, health and social care for young people with special educational needs or disabilities. This information is available on the local authority's website. For example, Camden Council's Local Offer can be found at www.localoffer.camden.gov.uk.

## Mantra Lingua

A UK based publishing company producing sound enabled books and resources. The company aims to increase accessibility to learning for young people with SEN. Founder members of the British Assistive Technology Association, the company has created a range of assistive technologies products catering for young people with additional communication, learning and interaction needs.

www.uk.mantralingua/sen

## Mencap

A charity working in partnership with people with a learning disability that provides services to support people to live how they choose. Provides information and advice for people with learning disabilities, families and carers. The website has an easy version for people with learning disabilities accessed from the main website via a blue button in the top right.

www.mencap.org.uk

## Mind

Mental health charity. Mental Capacity Act 2005 information is accessed by clicking: Information & Support, then Legal Rights, then MCA.

www.mind.org.uk

## MindEd

Provides free mental health e-learning and advice for all adults with a duty of care for children and young people.

www.minded.org.uk; Twitter account: https://twitter.com/MindEdUK

## National Autistic Society

A charity for people with autism. It provides information, support, pioneering services and campaigns for a better world for people with autism.

www.autism.org.uk

## National Children's Bureau

A charity that works with and for children to influence government policy, to provide creative solutions on a range of issues.

www.ncb.org.uk

## National Development Team for inclusion

Not-for-profit organisation concerned with promoting inclusion and equality for people who risk exclusion and who need support to lead a full life. Particular interests are issues around age, disability, mental health, children and young people.

www.ndti.org.uk

## National Sensory Impairment Partnership

A partnership of organisations working together to improve outcomes for children and young people with sensory impairments. The website offers a wide range of resources related to sensory impairment.

www.natsip.org.uk

## Tactile Talk Technology™ (PENpal)

A digital reader enables information to be recorded and replayed when the tip is placed on a micro-bar code. This enables someone who has difficulties accessing written materials to 'read' the page. Produced by Mantra Lingua.

      www.mantralingua.com

## POhWER

A charity and membership organisation. It provides information, advice, support and advocacy to people who experience disability, vulnerability, distress and social exclusion. An advocacy service is free, independent and confidential.

      www.pohwer.net

## Preparing for Adulthood

The Preparing for Adulthood programme is funded by the DfE as part of the delivery of and support for the SEN and disability reforms. The programme provides knowledge and support to all local authorities and their partners, including families and young people, so they can ensure that young people with special educational needs and disabilities achieve paid work, independent living, good health and community inclusion as they move into adulthood. The Programme has three strands of work: best practice and information sharing, wider support for all local areas and pathfinder support.

      www.preparingforadulthood.org.uk

## Proloquo2

An app for iOS operated devices (iPad) described as an augmentative and alternative communication system for young people who need symbol support to communicate. It has been successfully used with young people with a range of developmental disabilities and autism. It can be downloaded from Apple App store.

www.assistiveware.com/product/proloquo2go

## Rethink Mental Illness

This mental health charity helps by challenging attitudes and changing lives and policy. It directly supports people through crises and to live independently. It offers advice and information.

www.rethink.org.uk

## Royal College of Psychiatrists

Although this is the professional and education organisation for psychiatrists in the UK, it does produce materials for the general public about a range of mental health issues. It hosts an access to the MindEd website and also has its own app, RCP Psych App, giving instant access to leaflets and other information. There is information for parents and young people. Education professionals are likely to find the leaflets on a range of mental health issues helpful.

www.rcpsych.ac.uk

## Royal National Institute for the Blind (RNIB)

A charity supporting people with sight loss, providing advice and products to enable independence.

www.rnib.org.uk

## SANE

A mental health charity working to improve the lives of anyone affected by mental illness. It aims to raise public awareness and combat stigma. It provides care and support for people with mental health problems, their families and carers.

> www.sane.org.uk

## Sense

A charity supporting and campaigning for children and adults who are deaf/blind or who have sensory impairments.

> www.sense.org.uk

## Scope

A charity providing support, information and advice to disabled people and their families.

> www.scope.org.uk

## Social Care Institute for Excellence (SCIE)

Independent charity working with adults, families and children's care and support services across the UK. Produces freely available resources to improve the knowledge, skills and practice of care staff and commissioners.

> www.scie.org.uk

## Talking Mats™

A communication tool that uses a mat and picture symbols to facilitate young people with communication difficulties being able to express their views. To use Talking Mats a young person's language understanding needs to be at the two information-carrying words or above (Mackay and Murphy 2012).

    www.talkingmats.com

## Together

A national charity working alongside people with mental health issues. It offers personalised community support, safe housing and advocacy.

    www.together-uk.org

## The National Elf Service

Aims to bring the latest evidence-based research each week in the areas of mental health, learning disabilities and education.

    www.nationalelfservice.net (mental health and learning disabilities) or www.educationelf.net

## Young Minds

A child and adolescent mental health charity committed to improving the emotional wellbeing and mental health of children and young people.

    www.youngminds.org.uk

# Index

Page numbers in italic refer to figures and tables.

acquired brain injury 71
adoption 87
'adult', definitions 20, 24
American Psychiatric Association (APA) 69–70
assessors
   attributes 81–9
   considerations 78–81
   definition 193
   factors to be considered by 82
   who should assess? 75–8
Atkinson, C. 134, 137
attention issues 66, 67, 82, 86, 92
autism 72, 179
autonomy, right to 19, 32–3, 52–3, 130, 136

'best interests' 29, 36–7, 45–6, 107, 151–68, 173, 182, 183, 191, 193
   checklist 155–60, *155*, 193
   parental decisions 161–2
   resolving disputes with parents 163–7
brain injury, acquired 71
British Medical Association 81
British Psychological Society (BPS) 69, 90, 129–30, 131, 132, 133, 134–6, 138, 139, 163, 164
Brown, H. 190–1
'buddies' 22, 24

capacity
   assessment *see* capacity assessment
   definitions 12–13, 51–2, 194
   and EHC Plans 55–6
   lack of 54–5, 136, 147, 194
   presumption of 16, 20, 22, 31, 32–3, 37, 49, 52, 75, 111, 115–16, 133, 191
   types of decisions *see* 'everyday' decisions; 'legal consequences' decisions; 'more serious or significant' decisions
capacity assessment 13–14
   definitions 62–3, 193
   'four key questions' 63–71, 98–110
   guide to undertaking assessments 73–112
      assessors: attributes 81–9, *82*
      assessors: considerations 78–81
      assessors: who should assess? 75–8
      considerations when planning 89–97
      does the young person have capacity to make the decision 110–11
      frequency of assessment 111–12
      is an assessment necessary? 73–4, *74*
      using the 'four key questions' 98–110
   resolving disputes 145–50
      proposed resolution process 146–9
   summary of findings 71–2
   timescale 138–9
Care Quality Commission 190
case friends 16
challenging behaviour 40, 70
Chambers and Partners 149
change, dislike of 88
Chief Medical Officer 68
'child', definition 24

Children Act 1989 23, *25*
Children Act 2004 *25*
Children and Families Act 2014 15, 16, 19–20, 23, *26*, 29, 38, 41, 45, 52, 66, 67, 76, 115–16, 130, 132, 151, 152, 163, 169, 187, 193
  definition of 'young person' 20, 21, 24
Circles of Support 174, 181
civil partnerships 87
clinical psychologists 72, 78, 129, 130, 131, 132, 133–4, 136, 138, 139, 140
codes of practice (COP)
  definition 193
  see also MCA COP; SEND COP
collaborative working 77, 92–4, 105
communication issues see language and communication issues
concentration issues 69, 86, 92
Coram Children's Legal Centre 149
Council for Disabled Children 172–3
Court of Protection 14, 40, 45–8, 63, 111, 149, 166, 167, 193
  [2014] EWCOP 38 35, 48
cultural considerations, and capacity assessments 86–7
cyberbullying 71

decision-makers, definition 194
decisions, types of see 'everyday' decisions; 'legal consequences' decisions; 'more serious or significant' decisions
Department for Education (DfE) 12, 44–5, 62, 66, 67–8, 72
Department for Works and Pensions (DWP) 45
Department of Health 19, 30, 45, 65, 66, 71, 72, 81, 172, 177, *178*
deprivation of liberty 38–40, 40–3, 53, 194
Deprivation of Liberty Safeguards (DoLS) 30, 38, 190
diabetes 86
Down's syndrome 31
  see also 'Jill' scenarios

Down's Syndrome Association 172
Dunsmuir, S. 134, 137

Education, Health and Care (EHC) Plans
  'best interests' 151–2, 156
  and capacity 55–6, 62
  decision-making 20, 37, 53, 62, 75–6, 79, 157, 170, 175, 188, 189–90
  definition 194
  and extracurricular and social activities 21–4
  'Jill' scenarios 36, 109–10
  Law Society guidance 39
  and learning issues 66
  and the local authority 44, 102, 103–5
  parents and 161, 166, 170
  sections 103–5, *103*
  see also Special Educational Needs and Disability (SEND) Tribunal
Education Law Association 149
educational establishments, choosing new 89, 117, 182–3, 188, 190
  see also 'Jill' scenarios
educational psychologists (EPs) 78, 96, 129–41, 159, 165
  considerations for 133–9
  assessment approaches and time 138–9
  ethical and professional issues 135–-6
  service guidance 136–7
  understanding the MCA, training and access to information 133–5
  role in assessing capacity 130–3
EHC Plans see Education, Health and Care (EHC) Plans
emotional wellbeing issues 70–1
epilepsy 86
Equality Act 2010 21, 22, *25*, *26*
equipment, for capacity assessments 95–6
ethical issues 78, 135–6, 136

# Index

'everyday' decisions 37, 52–3, 54, 176, 178, 179–81, 184
extracurricular and social activities 21–4, 41, 53–4, 160, 162

Fletcher, I. 130, 131, 131–2, 133, 134, 136, 136–7, 138, 139, 140
foster care 38, 39, 46, 173
Fox, M. 130
further education (FE) colleges
  definition 194
  legal frameworks 25, 26
  out-of-district 89
  see also 'Jill' scenarios

Headway 71
hearing issues 70, 96, 122
human rights 14, 32
Human Rights Act 1998 25, 26

Impartial information, advice and support services 146, 148, 165
Independent, The 35
Independent Mental Capacity Advocates (IMCAs) 45
information
  access to for EPs 133–5
  and capacity assessments 85, 88–9, 106–7, 107–10
  conveying to parents 177
  Impartial information, advice and support services 146, 148, 165
International Classification of Diseases (ICD) 65, 67
iPads see 'Jill' scenarios; tablet computers

'Jill' scenarios 33–4, 35–6, 41–3, 46–8, 83–5, 92–4, 98–9, 101–2, 108–10, 119–20, 122, 156–7, 158, 159, 160, 162, 179

Lang, J. 134, 137
language and communication issues 33, 51, 55, 77, 82, 83–5, 92–3, 96, 97, 110, 126, 147
Law Commission 30

Law Society 38, 39–40, 41, 43, 134, 135, 190
learning difficulties and disabilities (LDD), definitions 65–7
'legal consequences' decisions 53, 111–12, 113, 177
  appealing to the SEND Tribunal 115–27
liberty, deprivation of see deprivation of liberty
local authorities, understanding the concept of 77, 79, 102, 105–6, 109, 140, 189–90
local authority officers 44, 75–6, 76–7, 80–1, 92–4, 105–6, 108–10
Local Offers 89, 146, 194

MCA COP 13, 45, 46, 173, 174–5, 176–7, 182, 187, 191
  Chapter 1 87, 132
  Chapter 2 33, 96, 116
  Chapter 3 33, 83, 88, 102–3
  Chapter 4 14, 31–2, 52–3, 54–5, 62–5, 71, 75–6, 78, 80–1, 87, 88–9, 95, 99, 100, 101–2, 106, 110, 112, 116, 130–1, 145–6, 147, 153
  Chapter 5 37, 52, 152–3, 155–6, 157, 163–4
  Chapter 6 80
  Chapter 13 30
  Chapter 15 146
  relationship to the SEND COP 12, 29, 32, 43–4, 71–2, 172, 176
Mackay, M.A. 241
Makaton see 'Jill' scenarios
Mantra Lingua 154, 177
Marchant, L. 190–1
marriage 87, 132
medical issues 45, 53, 86, 87
Medical Protection Society 35
memory aids 87, 106–7, 147, 154, 180, 182, 183, 190
  see also 'Jill' scenarios; language and communication issues
memory issues 51, 55, 69, 82, 83, 86, 106–7, 109
Mencap 154, 155
mental capacity see capacity

Mental Capacity Act 2005 25, 26,
    78–9, 81–2, 117, 120, 195
  Code of Practice see MCA COP
  definition 31–2
  five principles 29–30, 32–43, 46,
      55, 80, 81, 99, 175, *178*
    1: presumption of capacity 16,
        20, 22, 31, 32–3, 37, 49, 52,
        75, 111, 115–16, 133, 191
    2: individuals being supported
        to make their own
        decisions 33–4, 78, 81,
        86, 92, 105–6, 111, 175
    3: unwise decisions 34–6, 48
    4: 'best interests' see 'best interests'
    5: less restrictive option 37–43
  background 29–30
Mental Health Foundation 68, 90
mental health issues 67–70, 71, 72, 157
MindEd 69, 72
Mitchell, W. 169, 170–2, 179
'more serious or significant'
    decisions 53, 54, 176, 181–3
  see also capacity assessment
Murphy, J. 241

National Autistic Society 179
National Children's Bureau 70–1, 72
National Development Team for
    Inclusion (NDTI) 173
National Sensory Impairment
    Partnership (NatSIP) 29–30, 99
National Youth Advocacy
    Service (NYAS) 149
Newton, Sir Isaac 164
NVDA software 172

Oxford Reference 11

parents
  definition of 'parent' 195
  quotes by 19
  resolving disputes with 163–7
  supporting and working with 169–84
    'best interests' 161–2, 183
    concepts and terms associated
        with the MCA 174–7, *178*
    conveying information
        to parents 177
    making decisions 178–83
PENpal 154, 177
person-centred plans 88, 111, 157
personal budgets 44, 53, 75,
    77, 94, 105, 187, 195
Preparing for Adulthood
    programme 30, 172
Protective Care 30
psychiatrists 72, 78
  see also Royal College of
      Psychiatrists
psychologists see British Psychological
    Society; clinical psychologists;
    educational psychologists

record keeping 80, 98, 99,
    112, 131, 137, 161
residential settings 30, 38, 39, 40,
    41, 43, 46, 93, 171, 173
risk assessments 54
Royal College of Psychiatrists
    68, 69, 72, 129–30

safeguarding issues 166, 173
  see also deprivation of liberty
'Sam' scenarios 21–4, 54
scenarios see 'Jill' scenarios;
    'Sam' scenarios
school age, compulsory 20–1, 193
SCIE (Social Care Institute for
    Excellence) see Social Care
    Institute for Excellence
Seldon, J. 11
SEND COP 11–12, 15
  Annex 1 11–12, 13, 29, 32, 37, 62–3,
      76, 111–12, 130, 132, 151, 191
  APDR model 32
  and decision-making 37, 65, 108,
      151, 157, 169–70, 187, 189
  and EHC Plans 45, 75, 103, *103*
  emotional wellbeing issues 70
  legal status issues 20–1, 174–5
  and Local Offers 89
  and 'mental capacity' 13
  mental health issues 68

relationship to the MCA COP
29, 43–5, 52, 65–6, 71, 176
resolution of disagreements 146
Tribunal appeals 116, 116–17
service users, definition 195
sexual relations 35, 87, 132
sight issues 70, 96, 122
Sinson, J. 29–30, 172
Skype 77, 94, 165
social activities *see* extracurricular and social activities
Social Care Institute for Excellence (SCIE) 34, 81, 90, 129, 137, 139, 154
social media, misuse 70
*Special Educational Needs and Disability Code of Practice* see SEND COP
Special Educational Needs and Disability (SEND) Tribunal 45, 46, 53, 63, 104, 105, 115–27, 132, 146, 152, 166, 195
  capacity to bring an appeal 117–18
  the decision giving rise to the appeal 118–24
  Tribunal process 124–6
speech and language therapists 78, 96, 159
support
  during capacity assessments 96–7
  Impartial information, advice and support services 146, 148, 165
  *see also under* parents
Supreme Court, [2014] UKSC 19 30, 38–9, 53, 134, 179, 180, 190

tablet computers 33, 85, 95, 96
  *see also* 'Jill' scenarios
Talking Mats™ 107
Tactile Talk Technology™ 154, 177
teaching assistants (TAs) 22
Thunder software 172
training issues 72, 81, 133–5, 172, 173
Transitions Pathways Preparation for Adulthood 173
Tribunal Wales (Education) 16

United Nations (UN) 20, *25*

visual information *see* memory aids
VOIP 77, 165

Wales, legislation in 15–16
Walji, I. 130, 131, 131–2, 133, 134, 136, 136–7, 138, 139, 140
Weare, K. 70–1
Weatherhead, S. 130, 131, 131–2, 133, 134, 136, 136–7, 138, 139, 140
Welsh Government 15–16
Wright, S. 134, 137

Young Minds 68, 69, 72
young people
  age and the law conundrum 20–6, *25*
  definitions of 'young person' 20–1, 24, 174–5, 195
  developing decision-making ability 187–90